THE
IDEOLOGICAL
IMAGINATION

ALSO BY LOUIS J. HALLE

Transcaribbean
Birds against Men
River of Ruins
Spring in Washington
On Facing the World
Civilization and Foreign Policy
Choice for Survival
Dream and Reality
Men and Nations
Sedge
The Society of Man
The Cold War as History
The Storm Petrel and the Owl of Athena

LOUIS J. HALLE: THE IDEOLOGICAL IMAGINATION

QUADRANGLE BOOKS   CHICAGO · 1972

121
Halle

Library of Congress Catalog Card Number:
70-152093

SBN 8129-0195-9

The thoughts contained in this essay cannot have any other aim or effect upon publication than the understanding of that which is, and thus to promote calmer contemplation as well as the ability to endure it. . . .

HEGEL

Preface

IT WAS never my intention to write a treatise on ideology. All I had in mind was to follow up certain thoughts that had been developing in my head, and this is what I have done.

Where writing is a matter of following up thoughts it generally takes its own way. Beginning this essay (after the introductory material) with an account of normative thinking in the sixteenth and seventeenth centuries, I had a fair idea of the course it would follow until it got up to our present, but I could not tell what it would do then. What it did then was to become something like a tract for the times, concluding with a statement of personal philosophy. I am not sorry about this. It seems to me good that, if I was going to write this sort of thing, it should come at the end of an historical account that puts it into perspective.

No one who simply develops his own ideas on paper can properly regard them as absolutely true, or hope to escape error altogether. Speculation itself accepts the possibility of error, for it would not otherwise be speculation. The writer's obligation is to make as sure as he can of everything he says, not relying on secondhand information when he can go to the source, not misinterpreting the writers he cites, not being glib. He must also go over and over every sentence until all suppressed doubts have at last risen to the surface, and revise accordingly. I claim a right to be wrong, especially in speculative opinions, but no right to be irresponsible.

What I can assure the reader is that, in the words of St. Augustine of Hippo, "all this is therefore in some respects true, as it is in some respects false."

Let me return to my statement that a writer must not misinterpret others whom he cites or rely on secondhand information when he can go to the source. Rousseau should pose virtually no problem. He wrote with exemplary clarity, and I read him in the original French. I would have thought it almost beyond question that in his two "discourses" he upheld anarchism as an ideal (although recognizing that it could not be realized), that his *Social Contract* presents the model of a totalitarian state, that in many of his writings he showed himself to be a confused and aimless dreamer, and that the self-portrait in his *Confessions* and in much of his correspondence is that of an extreme sentimentalist whose sentimentalism might on occasion be vicious in its consequences. Yet I find so eminent a scholar as Professor Peter Gay referring to "the most surprising charges" of which Rousseau has been the victim, charges that have created the false popular conception of "Rousseau the anarchist, Rousseau the father of collectivist totalitarianism, Rousseau the confused aimless dreamer, Rousseau the vicious sentimentalist. . . ."[1] I am sorry. Professor Gay knows the background of Rousseau and the critical literature better than I do, and represents a magisterial authority I am bound to respect; but I must report what I myself find in Rousseau, after reading him over and over, even if it is at odds with such authority. The point is that Professor Gay would, I assume, say I had misinterpreted Rousseau.

If, then, such a problem of interpretation arises with a writer as limpid as Rousseau, how much greater is the problem posed by Hegel! Because Hegel hid much of his thought in a wrapping of impenetrable language, and because much of it is

---

[1] Introduction to Cassirer, p. xi. For full citations of all footnote references, see List of Publications, the last section of this book.

available only in the edited lecture notes of his students, it is directly accessible only in part, and then only to those who read German well and are prepared to spend years in what amounts to detective work on his writings or on what passes for them. It is not surprising if those who have done this do not agree among themselves on what Hegel thought.

Unhappily, I do not read German, but those who do tell me that Hegel is more obscure in the original than in translation. This is to be expected, because a translator makes what sense he can of passages that may have no determinable sense at all, translating accordingly. It follows, however, that the sense in the translation may not be Hegel's sense. The relative clarity of the translation is a false clarity.

It was my good fortune that a notable Hegel scholar, Professor Walter Kaufmann of Princeton, came for a visit to the chalet in the Alps where I was writing this essay. He read what I had written about Hegel, as it then was. In the course of climbing a mountain together, and through a long evening, he strove with patience and good humor to make me understand why what I had written was wrong or misleading. I resisted at first, struggling briefly like a butterfly being pinned by a collector. I pointed out what writers more or less eminent had said about what Hegel thought, whereupon he proceeded to persuade me that they were wrong. Then, with short-lived triumph, I quoted Hegel himself, albeit in translation. But it transpired that the translations I quoted were wrong. For example, I quoted from J. Sibree's 1857 translation of *The Philosophy of Right* the much quoted statement: "The march of God in the world, that is what the State is." Here is what Kaufmann has written about this bit of translation: ". . . the original says merely that it is the way of God with the world that there should be the State, and even this sentence is lacking in the text published by Hegel and comes from one of the editor's additions to the posthumous edition of *The Philosophy of Right*—and the editor admitted in

his Preface that, though these additions were based on lecture notes, 'the choice of words' was sometimes his rather than Hegel's."[1]

I had already twice read, albeit some years back, the 465 pages of Kaufmann's book on Hegel[2] (including his translation of, and commentary on, the Preface of *The Phenomenology of Mind*), filling its margins with my penciled notes; and after his visit I proceeded to go through it a third time, as well as to read the chapters on Hegel in *The Owl and the Nightingale*. Then I saw how he had saved me from falling into the errors of most commentators on Hegel, including some as eminent as Bertrand Russell and Sir Karl Popper, not to mention Karl Marx. Having been convinced of this, I proceeded to rewrite my brief passages on Hegel completely. Professor Kaufmann cannot be held responsible for the revised version, which he might wish to qualify with some fine print, but I cannot forbear to express my gratitude for the suffering he inflicted and the extra trouble he thereby moved me to take.

I mention this extreme case at a length it does not deserve in itself (since there are only three or four pages on Hegel in this book), simply to show that it is sometimes hard to be sure that one is following the rule of never misinterpreting other writers. In fact, almost all philosophical writers are regularly misinterpreted, often out of extreme carelessness, often by those whose names bear authority. I repeat, then, the distinction I have already made between being wrong and being irresponsible. It applies not only to one's own speculation in the realm of ideas but to much else besides. In this imperfect world one must do the best one can. Given the limitations of time, energy, and circumstances, that is what I have done here.

L. J. H.

Geneva, 1971

---

[1] Kaufmann, 1959, p. 91.   [2] Kaufmann, 1966.

Acknowledgements

I AM GRATEFUL to the many persons who have generously helped track down citations, locate translated passages in the original languages, and find other items of information. I do not list them here only because I would not know where to stop.

Miss Ulrike Wuttig's contribution deserves special recognition. Appendix II and the List of Publications are her work more than mine. While I went off to explore Antarctica during the austral summer of 1970–1971, she conducted research expeditions through the libraries of Geneva, or bearded scholarly experts in their dens to unearth citations and check translations. She is also the author of the Index. It takes a vast amount of painstaking and intelligent work to produce a good index, and hers is good. I am sure there must be a special place for good indexers in Heaven, because they so rarely have their reward here on earth.

L. J. H.

Contents

THE
IDEOLOGICAL
IMAGINATION

1

The GREAT international conflicts of the twentieth century have presented themselves in two guises: as conflicts between sovereign states and as conflicts between ideologies. This duality has been reflected in the identification of the enemy by the participants in conflict. For the victorious allies in World War II, the enemy might be identified as Germany, Italy, and Japan, or it might be identified as fascism. In the Cold War it has been Russia or communism.

This is not to say that the identification of the enemy has to be either one or the other, or even that it may not be something else altogether. Russia and communism have been associated together in men's minds, but the association has varied widely in emphasis on the one or the other. This is important because, in the great conflicts of our century, the way in which the enemy has been identified has determined how war and peace were made.

In the conclusion of World War II, Russian power expanded over half Europe, and communism along with it. The Cold War began when the United States decided to block any further expansion, to "contain" the expansion at the point it had already reached. The author of the containment policy, George Kennan, defined it as the "containment of Russian expansive tendencies."[1] With the passage of time, however, this was imperceptibly transmuted, in the common mind, until what had begun as the containment of "Russian expansive tendencies" became the containment of communism. So the United States

[1] Kennan, 1947.

3

found itself containing China and North Vietnam as well as Russia, if only on the assumption that all communist expansion was Russian expansion.

A state is easier to define than an ideology. Virtually any literate adult, asked what the word "Russia" means, could reply in precisely delimiting terms. Asked what "communism" means, his answer would probably be vague, confused, and without clearly delimiting terms. In actual practice, he would probably identify as communist whatever called itself that. Although there is reason to believe that, while the Russian government regarded Mao Tse-tung, from 1927 on, as not a real but an imitation communist, the American people had no doubt that he was a real communist and that his regime was a real communist regime because they went by the label.

The problem of definition that the word "communism" poses is also posed by "fascism," the name of the other great ideology with which half the world has been in conflict. Therefore, if an ideology is something more than a name, as it surely is, the question of what it is arises.

In a simple view, the ideology called communism was the brainchild of Karl Marx, originally presented to the world in the *Manifesto of the Communist Party* in 1848. Therefore one turns to the *Manifesto* to find out what it is. What one discovers, however, is that the *Manifesto* contains predictions which have not been fulfilled, that it describes a proletarian revolution which has taken place nowhere (neither the Russian Revolution of 1917 nor the Chinese Revolution of 1949 even remotely fits the description), and that it depicts a post-revolutionary society which corresponds to little in Russia, in China, in North Vietnam, in Cuba, or in any other country that calls itself communist. Little of what Marx advocated in the entire body of his writings corresponds to anything in the societies that have labeled themselves communist and have claimed to represent what he stood for.

One may answer that communism is an evolving system of belief, or an evolving design for society. It has undergone a constant development that, by the accumulation of change with time, has at last come to represent something quite different from what Marx projected, but with which it is nevertheless connected by the unbroken line of its development. In the same way, although I now appear different from what I was at birth, I am still the same person.

Within its limits, this seems to me valid. Everything changes with time, states and ideologies alike. What we call "France" today is quite different from what was called "France" in the fifteenth century, but a continuous development connects the two.

The development of a body of belief, however, or of a design for society, is never along one line only. It branches. This has been the case with Marxism, as witness the fact that the Russian Communists and the German Social Democrats of our day alike claim for their respective doctrines descent from the doctrine of Marx, although they differ widely. Is it not possible that the "communism" of Russia and the "communism" of China, while bearing the same name, are also different and opposed? If so, then those of us who identify all movements that bear the communist label as the same movement have mistaken the nominal for the real, with far-reaching consequences. The war in Vietnam would be one of these consequences.

The word "ideology" has a wide range of meanings that, like all words denoting abstractions, has changed over the generations. I do not use it here in its widest sense, to denote any complex of ideas whatever. For one thing, I confine it to bodies of doctrine that present themselves as affording systems of belief so complete that whole populations may live by them alone, that are made known and interpreted by leaders ostensibly possessed of special genius or by organized élites not unlike priesthoods,

that claim exclusive authority as representing something like revealed truth, and that consequently require the suppression of whatever does not conform. Perhaps I should put it that I am concerned here only with systems of belief that are implicitly totalitarian.

It will be seen that "ideology," so defined, not only excludes liberal democracy but is its opposite. For liberal democracy is based on the assumption that none of us mortals have a privileged knowledge of truth, that equally honest and intelligent men will disagree in their identification of it. Therefore, instead of undertaking to abolish diversity it seeks to accommodate it, providing an open marketplace in which men of varying beliefs may compete in offering their intellectual wares to the public. Such a marketplace, in order to accommodate diversity, requires freedom of speech and mutual tolerance.

My use of the term "ideology," as I have defined it so far, does not exclude organized religions like Christianity. However, although the European society of the Middle Ages was based on an exclusive and intolerant Christianity, just as Russian society today is based on an exclusive and intolerant communism, no important society of our times is thus based on any traditional religion. Since I am concerned here only with the ideologies that have played such a dominant role in the world since the French Revolution, I exclude the world's ancient religions, all of which differ from modern ideologies by their claim to supernatural authority and to knowledge of a supernatural world.

Beyond this I am not categorical in my definition. There are all sorts of vague terms that refer to vague bodies of ideological belief, or merely to intellectual attitudes, such as "the left," "the new left," "the radical right," and so forth. To the extent that a phenomenon is not well defined in itself it defies definition in words. This is true to some extent of the great ideologies, but especially true of whatever may be represented by names like those I have just cited.

I am concerned with the role of ideology in the modern world. To be precise, I am concerned with the role of ideology in a world, inaugurated by the French Revolution, in which political sovereignty is attributed to the people rather than to individual rulers. If I define democracy as the attribution of sovereignty to the people, then there is a close historical association between the development of democracy and the development of ideology. Where the political activity of whole populations has to be taken into account, ideology provides the basis of a common mind, at the same time that it provides, as well, a means by which one or a few men can manipulate multitudes. It serves a purpose that would not have been relevant to the earlier societies in which sovereignty was vested in individual rulers while the populations ruled by them remained politically inert and obedient.

Ideology and democracy, then, go together. The history of ideology goes together with the history of democracy. I shall therefore be examining ideology, for the most part, as an historical phenomenon.

2

Is it possible that the United States, in the late 1960's, was fighting communism in Southeast Asia without knowing what communism was? Hundreds of millions of lives have been sacrificed in this century to fight what? Communism? Fascism? Imperialism? Russia? China? Germany? Japan? What are these nominal entities that we combat at the cost of so much human suffering and destruction?

When we try to answer this question we may easily gain the impression that the nations of the world are constantly engaged in fighting mere shadows. Surely, however, it is inconceivable that they pour out their blood and treasure to fight shadows.

Surely the Atlantic nations were fighting a real menace from 1939 to 1945. Surely these same nations were again opposing a real menace when they embarked on the policy of containment in 1947, although it is so hard to be clear on what they were containing.

The fact is that the international world is one in which realities and mythical conceptions are all mixed up together. The realities are largely unknown, even to the most knowledgeable among us, and so we make myths surrogates for them. In the darkness of our ignorance we half see shapes that our imagination then transforms into all sorts of things that they may or may not be. We half see something that we call fascism, or communism, or capitalism, or imperialism, and in our imagination we proceed to endow it with a variety of attributes. We can hardly tell what is real and what imaginary in the great world with which we are dealing when we address ourselves to international relations, the great world that extends so far beyond what we can see with our own eyes.

Those who are best informed among us recognize today that the "monolithic communist empire" in which we believed in the 1950's, the empire ruled by Moscow of which Mao Tse-tung and Ho Chi Minh were obedient agents, was a myth. Those who are best informed recognize today that in May 1950, when the American Secretary of State announced that the United States was intervening in Vietnam to prevent "Soviet imperialism" from establishing its domination there, he was speaking, and the United States was acting, in terms of a myth that did not correspond to reality. Inevitably this arouses the question to what extent we may all be thinking and acting today on the basis of myths that do not correspond to reality.

The confusion between myth and reality is most poignant when, in the midst of conflict, it comes to the identification of one's enemy. We may think that the difficulty of definition we run into when we identify the enemy as an ideology, like

communism, does not arise when we identify it as a state, like the Soviet Union. But it does, as a couple of historical examples will show.

In 1815, when the Napoleonic Wars ended and the victors rode in triumph through the streets of Paris, the question of imposing a settlement on the defeated enemy came up. But who, or what, was the defeated enemy? Was it a Corsican adventurer called Napoleon Bonaparte? Or was it the French nation as it had emerged from the French Revolution, a single society composed of all its citizens? If the enemy was simply the man Bonaparte, then a sensible settlement might be to imprison him on an island in the South Atlantic, to restore the legitimate Bourbon ruler whose place he had usurped, and then to re-establish normal relations with the restored ruler. However, if the enemy was the French nation, or people, then the problem of what kind of settlement to make would be altogether different. It would not be possible to transfer the whole French people to St. Helena; and even if it were possible, the problem of what to put in its place would arise.

It was because the victors of 1815 identified the enemy as Bonaparte that they were able to make a real peace. At the conclusion of World War I, despite Woodrow Wilson's original insistence that the enemy was the Kaiser's regime and not the German people, the identification of the enemy as "Germany," under whatever regime, precluded the making of a real peace.

Even if we identify the enemy in the Cold War as Russia or the Soviet Union, rather than communism, we cannot be sure we know what we mean. In a history of the Cold War called *Struggle for the World*, Desmond Donnelly has it beginning in the middle of the nineteenth century, when the principal powers of western Europe were already engaged in a struggle to contain "Russian expansive tendencies." It follows that the Russia Mr. Donnelly regards as the object of containment is a traditional power the identity of which is independent of whatever kind of

regime or ideology may be governing it at a particular time. On the other hand, according to André Fontaine, in his history called *La Guerre Froide,* the Cold War began immediately after the Bolsheviks, in 1917, seized power. For him it is not the eternal Mother Russia but Communist Russia that has been the enemy and the objective of containment.

Is it too much to say that the fate of the world depends on how one identifies one's enemy?

If Russia under Stalin was still the age-old Russia continuing on its age-old course, and if China under Mao Tse-tung was still the age-old China continuing on its age-old course, then one might expect that the relations between these two powers would continue to be relations of confrontation and conflict, as they had been since the middle of the seventeenth century. On the other hand, if the old Russia had died in 1917, to be replaced by a new Russia, and if the old China had died in 1949, to be replaced by a new China, and if the two were to be identified by a common ideology that bound them together, then one might expect them to be united in a common cause against the traditional powers of the West.

Finally, even if one said that the enemy in the Cold War was the traditional Russia, could one be sure what one meant by "the traditional Russia"? Using the terminology of Jean-Jacques Rousseau, one might say that this Russia was a "political body" moved by a "general will." One might, in other words, regard it as a person, although a corporate rather than an individual person. The question would then arise whether a corporate person was a real person, or whether it was a myth; and if it was the latter the question would arise whether it was a myth that represented reality, fantasy, or a mixture that might have more or less of the one or the other.

These questions are philosophical, but the practical consequences that flow from their resolution are such that the history of mankind depends on it.

In the darkness of our common ignorance, shadowy shapes loom up ahead of us, and we can never be quite sure what to make of them. It is in such a scene that we conduct our international relations for better or for worse.

3

ESPECIALLY WHEN it comes to the elementary realities of this mundane sphere, we men know almost nothing as a matter of sure knowledge. Finding it virtually intolerable, however, to live in the vacuum of our own ignorance, we are driven to fill it with what passes for knowledge, whether in the form of a mythology that we take on faith or of a doctrinal system handed down to us from above by some pretended human authority like Karl Marx, or Adolf Hitler, or Mao Tse-tung. The true and almost unique greatness of Socrates lay in his recognition of his own and all men's ignorance. It is a depressing thought that not only was his agnosticism punished by his death twenty-four centuries ago, but the basic fact of our ignorance, and our consequent dependence on mythology, has continued to be covered up ever since.

If we take any simple and concrete object, say a table, we may apply our physical senses to know what it is. Looking at it with our eyes, feeling it with our fingers, hearing with our ears the sound it produces when we tap it, we conclude that it is solid, brown, hard, and so on. But the physicists of our day tell us something else about it that does not accord at all with the information derived through our senses. They say that it is composed of molecules, that the molecules are composed of atoms, and that the atoms are composed of particles that are not even material objects as we know them in the world of our senses.

The overwhelming preponderance of its volume is empty space (or space occupied by fields of force in which energy of one kind or another is propagated). Dynamic forces, enough to kill everyone for hundreds of miles around the table, hold its constituent elements together. This is not at all the table that our senses, on which we depended so confidently, presented to us. Neither, perhaps, is it the table that the physicists of some future generation will present to us.

If there is, then, a problem of knowing what a table is, how much greater a problem must there be of knowing anything as intangible as a state or an ideology, neither of which we can apprehend through our senses or even subject to examination through an electronic microscope. In what sense can we say even that it *is* at all?

I begin by asking a question: International relations are relations between what?

A simple answer would be that they are relations between states—states like France, Mexico, China, Sierra Leone. Such states as these are the actors in international relations. We attribute personality to them, saying of Spain, for example, that she looks back with nostalgia on her past grandeur, or saying of China that she resents the pretensions of Russia.

A man freshly arrived from Mars who heard us talking like this might ask to be presented to one of these actors in international relations.

How would we explain why we could not meet his wish?

We might say that, while a state has entity and personality of a sort, it is not a tangible physical reality like him or us. It doesn't exist physically in the sense that one can see it, hear it, smell it, taste it, or touch it.

This, however, says merely what a state is not. If each state is an actor, however, it follows that it must act. Since it acts purposefully, it must have a will to direct its action. What is the source of that will? Where is it located?

The locus of the state's will would have been easier to determine in the Europe of the sixteenth and seventeenth centuries than it is in the Europe of today. In Shakespeare's *King Henry V*, a tangible man, Henry of Lancaster, comes out on the stage, where he meets another tangible man, Charles of Valois. Says Henry to Charles: "Peace to this meeting, wherefore we are met! unto our brother France"—to which Charles replies: "Right joyous are we to behold your face, most worthy brother England." Here is a situation in which, it appears, France and England can actually behold each other's faces.

Under these circumstances "the will of France" was easily discovered to be in the physical person, Charles of Valois. It was his personal will when acting in his capacity as the sovereign of France; and "the will of England" was the personal will of Henry of Lancaster when acting as the sovereign of England. These two physical persons were absolute sovereigns. Each ruled over wide expanses of earth. Each ruled over multitudinous populations of which every member owed him obedience. Each had retainers or servants to carry out his will, the will of France or the will of England. Each had soldiers organized in companies and regiments to fight for him and enforce his will as France or England.

The case is different today; for, while Charles of Valois spoke *as* France, the President of France speaks merely *for* France. Charles was the sovereign of France, and his will was the sovereign will of France. But the President today is merely the spokesman for the sovereignty of France, which is lodged elsewhere than in his person. When he speaks for "the will of France" he is speaking for the will of some other person, whether tangible or intangible, as an ambassador might have spoken for the will of a king in earlier days.

The difference between the earlier time and the present is in the locus of sovereignty. In the twentieth century the sovereign, instead of being a visible person, is a putative entity called "the

people," which is not visible as such. "The will of France," in the modern theory of the state, is "the will of the French people." It is this change, from the dynastic state of earlier times to the nation-state of today, that has created the problem we face when the man from Mars says he would like to be presented to one of the actors in international relations.

"The people" is a corporate person and, as such, an abstraction. An abstraction cannot speak for itself. Someone else has to be spokesman for it, on whatever basis of authority. Josef Stalin spoke for "the will of the Soviet people"; Mao Tse-tung speaks for "the will of the Chinese people"; Richard Nixon speaks for "the will of the American people." It is the transfer in modern times of state sovereignty from a physical person to an abstraction that has created the problem to which all modern ideologies address themselves, each in its own way.

We commonly think of "international relations" as going back at least to the beginning of recorded history. The Greeks of the fifth century B.C. were organized in "city-states" rather than "nation-states," but we nevertheless think of the relations among their city-states as "international relations." We also think of the relations between the associated city-states of Greece, on the one hand, and the Persian Empire, on the other, as "international relations." It is therefore interesting to note that the first recorded use of the word "international," according to the *Oxford English Dictionary*, was in 1780, nine years before the French Revolution got under way. This is historically appropriate in terms of one of the definitions of "nation" that the dictionary gives: "the whole people of a country." (Later we shall see that even a definition as clear as this seems may have in it an element of equivocation, for "the whole people" cannot mean the whole population in the minds of those who, on ideological grounds, distinguish between "the people" and "the enemies of the people.")

When we say that "international relations" go back to the dawn of history, what we must mean is that relations between sovereign states, whatever their nature, go back to the dawn of history. We use the term loosely, projecting present normative conceptions on a past that, for the most part, knew them not.

In the period of history that followed the French Revolution sovereignty was transferred, in France and everywhere else, from a tangible physical person to an intangible, invisible entity called "the people." Today the sovereign of France is something called "the French people," which is, we must suppose, an abstraction, an idea, a conception in the mind. Although it may correspond directly or indirectly to some tangible reality, it is not such a reality in itself.

According to the modern theory of the state, "the will of France," for which its President speaks, is the will of the national entity called "the French people." It may be what Rousseau called "the general will," a term that he defined, as we shall see, in a sense different from that which we ourselves might give it at first thought.

Without deploring the transfer of sovereignty from an individual ruler to "the people"—indeed without passing any judgment on it at all—we may note a prime problem in political philosophy to which it gave rise. We may put it metaphorically by saying that, at the beginning of modern times, the scepter was wrested from the hands of an individual physical man with the purpose of putting it into the hands of "the people." But who has ever seen "the hands of the people"? Where are they? How does one find them?

As we shall see, various ideologies have given various answers to this question.

4

THE LATE EIGHTEENTH century is one of the watersheds in the history of political organization. Before it, legitimacy still appertained to the dynastic state with a physical person as sovereign; thereafter it came increasingly to be attached to the nation-state with a notional person as sovereign. The question arises: What is the authority that gives legitimacy to one kind of state rather than another?

James I of England maintained that the dynastic state, as represented by his realm, was the only proper kind of state. On what authority? The founders of the United States of America and their successors have repeatedly affirmed that its kind of liberal democracy is the only proper design for the state, to which the rest of the world must eventually come. On what authority? The leaders of the Soviet Union have insisted that it alone represents the proper design, a design which is therefore bound, as a matter of historical inevitability, to replace all other designs the world over. Again, on what authority?

People do not live within a state and accept its rule unless they feel that it represents the norm, the way things are supposed to be. They must feel that the kind of state they accept has legitimacy, which means that they must believe there is an ultimate authority of some kind for it. What authority?

Throughout much of history the authority invoked to legitimize a particular form of state has been God or nature. In his *Politics* Aristotle wrote: "It is evident that the city-state belongs to the class of things that exist by nature, and that man is by nature an animal intended to live in a city-state."[1] This is un-

[1] Aristotle, 1253 a.

convincing to those of us who, benefiting from broader experience than his, know the wide variety of social organization under which the human animal has actually lived. If, however, what he had written was that "man is by nature an animal intended to walk on two legs," we could hardly fail to agree; for the anatomy of man, which is a fact of nature, is suited only to bipedal locomotion. Again, if what Aristotle had said was that "the honeybee is by nature an animal intended to live in a hive," it would be hard to disagree; because for hundreds of thousands of years no honeybee has been able to survive at all except within the unchanging social organization of the hive.

By contrast with the honeybee, whatever man's ultimate destiny may be he has not yet evolved any form of social organization that could be called natural on the grounds that it represents a unique possibility, that there is no alternative to it. Yet the sanction of God or nature has been repeatedly invoked, since Aristotle, whenever there was need of ultimate authority to give legitimacy to a particular political design. So it is that the American Declaration of Independence, in its first sentence, justifies the revolt of the American colonists against their British sovereign by citing "the separate and equal station to which the Laws of Nature and of Nature's God entitle them."

The dynastic state likewise was justified by the claim that it had the authority of God. In *The Six Books of the Republic*, published in 1576, Jean Bodin wrote: "Because there is nothing greater on earth, after God, than the sovereign princes, and that they are established by him as his lieutenants, to rule over other men, it is necessary to have due regard for their status, so as to respect and obey their majesty in all obedience, and to speak of them in honorable terms: for whoever shows contempt for his sovereign prince shows contempt for God, of whom he is the image on earth."[1]

Since the days when Bodin claimed that King Henry III was

[1] Bodin, pp. 154–155.

absolute ruler of France by God's authority, we have lost the simple faith that made the divine right of kings plausible to their contemporaries. Most of us would regard Bodin's doctrine as an example of the kind of mythology that has been naively invoked throughout history to endow governments with the legitimacy on which the consent of the governed depends.

With the advent of the Renaissance there began an erosion of the faith that supported the divine right of kings. Francis Bacon, in the late sixteenth and early seventeenth centuries, began to substitute inductive thinking for the deductive thinking of theology. His younger contemporary, René Descartes, resumed the Socratic process of inquiry whereby one followed wherever the argument led, without regard for religious orthodoxy. By the middle of the eighteenth century this secularization of thinking had produced a spreading skepticism that undermined the myth of divine right and, along with it, the type of state which depended on the myth. As the dynastic state lost legitimacy there was bound to be increasing consideration of other types of state based on other authority than that of the myth, even if the other authority should be only another myth. The way was incidentally being prepared for the ideologies of the modern world.

We may think in terms of two watersheds. The transfer of sovereignty from the individual ruler to the people is one. The other is the corresponding development of a new myth (to be succeeded by others) in place of the divine right of kings. One of the pioneers in the development of this new myth was that contemporary of Bacon and Descartes, the author of *Leviathan*, Thomas Hobbes.

It would be hard to find a more convinced advocate of the rule of one physical person, with sovereignty vested in him, than Hobbes. At the same time, however, as a freethinker, a rationalist, a materialist, and a skeptic, he could hardly base his

advocacy on divine right. Therefore, while everything he wrote supported the absolute rule of one man, as it was known in practice to him and Bodin alike, he put forward a new and different myth to support it. That myth would prove subversive in a way he never intended it to be.

Aristotle had said, in effect, that just as it is the nature of honeybees to live in hives, so it is the nature of men to live in city-states. Hobbes's idea of what constituted the state of nature for man was something different. The state of nature, as he conceived it, was the state in which man had originally been before, departing from it, he had organized and entered into the state of civil society. It was the state of anarchy. It was, as he said in *Leviathan*, a state of war, "and such a war, as is of every man, against every man."

> In such condition [he wrote], there is no place for industry; because the fruit thereof is uncertain: and consequently no culture of the earth; no navigation, nor use of the commodities that may be imported by sea; no commodious building; no instruments of moving, and removing, such things as require much force; no knowledge of the face of the earth; no account of time; no arts; no letters, no society; and which is worst of all, continual fear, and danger of violent death; and the life of man, solitary, poor, nasty, brutish, and short.[1]

In Hobbes's conception, then, not only was there no divine authority for organized society, such a society was opposed to nature. In another famous passage he wrote: "This great Leviathan, which is called the State, is a work of art; it is an artificial man made for the protection and salvation of the natural man, to whom it is superior in grandeur and power."[2]

Here is the expression of a kind of political realism that marks the dawn of the modern age. The state, so far from being regarded as either divinely ordained or natural, is regarded as an artificial construction improvised by men as a means of escaping from their natural condition.

[1] Hobbes, Part I, Chap. 13, p. 82.
[2] Preface to the Latin edition of *Leviathan*.

This realism immediately opens the question of what authority there is for the state, or for any particular form of state. As a practical matter, the question has to be answered because people do not willingly accept the rule of the state unless they feel that it represents the way things are supposed to be in terms of some authority on a level above the questioning of ordinary mortals.

Hobbes, while eliminating the authority of God or nature, could not provide any other sufficient authority for the kind of state he espoused. A pragmatist as well as a realist, he viewed the state as simply a necessary evil. It was entirely man-made, a contraption by means of which men could escape from the intolerable condition in which they had previously found themselves. The authority for it, therefore, was nothing better than what would in later times be called positive law, the authority of a contractual arrangement to be respected not because God or nature underwrote it but because it served the general interest to respect it. In the same way, the evil practiced by Machiavelli's Prince had behind it no justification more inspiring than that of necessity: not to practice it would be worse.

If only to put this in symbolic terms, the positivistic Hobbes assumed that the state or, as he called it, the commonwealth, had been brought into existence by the conclusion of an actual contract into which men had at one time entered.

> A *commonwealth* [he wrote] is said to be *instituted*, when a multitude of men do agree, and *covenant, every one with every one,* that to whatsoever *man,* or *assembly of men,* shall be given by the major part, the *right* to *present* the person of them all, (that is to say, to be their *representative*); every one, as well he that *voted for it,* as he that *voted against it,* shall *authorize* all the actions and judgments, of that man, or assembly of men, in the same manner, as if they were his own, *to the end, to live peaceably amongst themselves, and be protected against other men.*

From this institution of a commonwealth are derived all the

rights, and *faculties* of him, or them, on whom the sovereign power is conferred by the consent of the people assembled.[1]

The reader will have noted that the "multitude of men" who, according to Hobbes, enter into a covenant, "every one with every one," do so in order to confer sovereignty on either a "man" or an "assembly of men." Further on in *Leviathan* he argues powerfully in favor of conferring it on one man rather than an assembly. He goes on to argue that the power conferred on the sovereign ruler is unlimited and irrevocable. The sovereign can command what he pleases, and his subjects are bound to obey (although there is an equivocal exception made for the right of self-defence when a subject's life is at issue). Finally, the individual sovereign being mortal, his sovereignty includes the power of deciding who his successor shall be. If he does not explicitly exercise this power, the supposition must be that, in accordance with custom, he has willed that the succession should fall on his next of kin.

Hobbes is not to be identified with the modern conception, formulated by Rousseau, of "the people" as a corporate person possessed of a "general will" and capable of acting in relation to other like corporate persons—capable, in fact, of itself exercising sovereignty. Hobbes was categorical in attaching the value of reality only to what manifests itself physically, and therefore in denying it to conceptual abstractions like that of the corporate person with the "general will." "The people," it follows, could not, like one physical person, be an actor in international relations.

A multitude of men [he wrote], are made *one* person, when they are by one man, or one person, represented; so that it be done with the consent of every one of that multitude in particular. For it is the *unity* of the representer, not the *unity* of the represented, that maketh the person *one*. And it is the representer that

[1] Hobbes, Part 2, Chap. 18, p. 113.

beareth the person, and but one person: and *unity*, cannot otherwise be understood in multitude.[1]

Hobbes was a conservative in his support of the absolute
monarchy that prevailed in his day. Even the idea of a social
contract was not in itself original with him, for in one or another
aspect it goes back to antiquity. He was, rather, a great and a
radical innovator in advancing the myth of social contract to
replace divine right as the authority on which the legitimacy of
the state rested. This, as many of his contemporaries understood, was bound to be subversive.

5

W HAT HOBBES substituted for the myth of divine right
was the myth of the social contract. He was certainly under no
illusion, himself, that there had ever been a day when all the
people of Britain had come together, like the barons on the
field of Runnymede, and by an act of perfect unanimity
instituted the monarchical state under which they still lived in
his time. We must think of him as saying, in effect, that it was *as
if* the people of Britain had done so, for they did in fact find
themselves bound by what could be regarded as a contractual
obligation.

By the myth of social contract Hobbes made the people,
rather than God, the original source of the absolute power that
the king exercised. Although he maintained that this power,
once given, could never be taken back, for political philosophers
after him it would be an easy step from this conception to the
conception that the continuing authority under which the king
held his rule was that of the people. And from this, in turn, it

[1] Hobbes, Part I, Chap. 16, p. 107.

would be no step at all to the conception that the people were sovereign.

After Hobbes, however, the attribution of sovereignty to the multitudinous people would pose a philosophical problem that had not existed when sovereignty was attributed to a single man. For how can the multitude all occupy the throne together and give commands? (The same problem, as we shall see, would arise with Karl Marx's projected dictatorship of the proletariat.) The state, at least as an actor in international relations, can have only one sovereign will. If the multitude of individual wills were ever identical, if there were ever unanimity among them, then such a single will might, for practical purposes, be said to exist. Hobbes compromised to the extent of accepting unanimity at one remove, qualifying the statement I quoted at the end of the last chapter when he came to describe "the act of instituting a commonwealth." "A *commonwealth*," he wrote, in the passage already quoted, "is said to be *instituted*, when a *multitude* of men do *agree, and covenant, every one with every one*, that to whatsoever *man* . . . shall be given by the major part, the *right* to *present* the person of them all . . .; every one, as well he that *voted for it*, as he that *voted against it*, shall *authorize* all the actions and judgments, of that man, . . . in the same manner, as if they were his own. . . ." In other words, as part of the myth of social contract he postulated unanimous agreement to accept the man chosen by a majority only as, nevertheless, the representative of all. After the unanimous constitutive action, which was mythically symbolic rather than historically real, and the subsequent election of an individual sovereign, nothing was left for the people but submission in perpetuity.

As I have observed, however, this is so close to popular sovereignty as almost to be popular sovereignty. The single ruler is chosen by majority vote and vested with "the *right* to *present* the person of them all, that is to say, to be their *representative*. . . ."

What is basic to popular sovereignty, real or pretended, is that the multitude do not themselves exercise it directly from hour to hour, but that it is so exercised by a single man or a group of men acting as their representative. Perhaps the king still sits by himself on the throne and issues the commands that his personal judgment dictates, but now he does so not as the chosen of God but as the representative of the people, in their name rather than his own. If there is always some element of make-believe in this, it is in some degree a necessary make-believe, for all the people cannot sit together on the throne and issue commands for themselves.

Again, popular sovereignty, real or pretended, has always had some resort to the equivocation of majority choice as a means of determining what is then represented as unanimous choice. The equivocation resides in the agreement, real or pretended, of those who are not of the majority to accept the will of the majority as the will of all, themselves included. By this kind of agreement on my part, albeit tacit, the President of the United States is authorized to speak for me even after I have voted against him and his policies. Although in literal truth he could never say that he spoke for other than a part of the American people on any particular issue, by the practice of an equivocal logic generally accepted he does in fact say that he speaks for the American people as an indivisible whole.

The wide scope for equivocation in the operations of any society based on popular sovereignty provides the setting for the ideologies of the modern world. Hobbes virtually established that setting, although he stopped just at the point of overtly attributing sovereignty to the people.

Perhaps one should put it that, according to the school of Bodin, the king was sovereign by the will of God, a mythic being with a mythic will. According to Hobbes, the king was sovereign by the will of the people, also a mythic being with a mythic will. According to those who came after Hobbes, the

people itself was the sovereign, although it still had to be represented as God had had to be represented, as it had had to be represented itself when the king had been sovereign only by its will.

It is evident that the word "sovereign," itself, is not without equivocation; and indeed the necessarily factitious character of any state makes it impossible to dispense with an element, more or less large, of equivocation—of falsehood, if one prefers the term. This is part of the dilemma of mankind in its present stage of evolution.

Everything I have said in this chapter has been based on Hobbes's conception of the people as plural rather than singular, as a multitude rather than a corporate person. For an important part of the political philosophers who came after him, however, simplifying abstractions like "the people" (singular) would have a more vivid reality than the multitudinous and multifarious individual phenomena of the visible world. This would be true of Rousseau, Hegel, and Marx, to come no closer to our present.

6

BEGINNING WITH Hobbes, two separate and opposed tendencies develop. One is the predominant Continenta tendency to design ideal models of society in terms of an abstract logic that takes little account of existential realities. The other is the predominant Anglo-Saxon tendency to recognize the limits imposed by existential realities and to do what can be done within them, even though it means sacrificing logic to workability.

I am aware of the simplification that my statement of this

distinction represents. The distinction, however, is nonetheless real. Let me illustrate it. Since Britain became a United Kingdom, England and Scotland have shared one monarch, who has been the head of the established church in each country. The fact that the English church is Anglo-Catholic (a term that is a contradiction in itself), the Scottish Presbyterian, is dealt with by having the monarch profess the one faith when south of the Tyne, the other when north of it. At least in make-believe, he undergoes a religious conversion every time he crosses the river. One can hardly imagine the French, in a similar situation, accepting anything so illogical, even though the price of not accepting it was religious war or the break-up of the state.

Since the state cannot be under a multitude of sovereigns, the implication of attributing sovereignty to the people is that the people are one. Hobbes, regarding the people as many, did not make them sovereign. After him, however, when popular sovereignty came to be the ruling conception, the problem of making them one, or of making them seem as one, had to be dealt with.

The predominantly Anglo-Saxon line of thought that represents liberal democracy, passing through John Locke and the makers of the American Revolution, accepts the fact of the many and improvises political machinery to derive unity by way of certain procedures that are necessarily arbitrary in some degree. Thus, within limits that represent acknowledged minority rights and the rights of those as yet unborn, the minority will accept the formal pretense of the magistrate elected by the majority to speak for all the people as if they were one. Accepting the principle of popular sovereignty, which implies one sovereign will that is "the will of the people," the members of the minority agree to the pretense whereby their votes are disregarded.

What liberal democracy does is to accept the fact of diversity

and seek to accommodate it. The other tradition, which it is convenient to call the Jacobin or totalitarian tradition, seeks to overcome diversity by the imposition of conformity. Jean-Jacques Rousseau may be regarded as the father of this other tradition, which is the tradition that leads to the ideologies of the twentieth century.

Rousseau, in *Of the Social Contract*, argued that the institution of a civil society by social contract required each of the individual persons constituting the people to abnegate his independence as an individual and, in his new capacity of citizen, assume the status of a cell in the body politic, no longer capable of functioning by himself. The social contract, he wrote, could be reduced to the following terms: "Each one of us contributes to the commonality his person and all his powers under the supreme direction of the general will; and we receive each member as an indivisible part of the whole." The provisions of the social contract, he said, amount to only one, which is "the total alienation of each associate with all his rights to the whole community."[1]

Rousseau was not given pause by the fact that this transformation of the independent individual into a cell of the body politic would require that he be denatured. "Whoever dares undertake to institute a people," he wrote, "must feel himself capable of changing human nature, so to speak, of transforming each individual, who by himself is a perfect and single whole, into part of a greater whole from which he somehow receives his life and his being; he must feel himself capable of altering man's constitution in order to reinforce it, of substituting a partial and moral existence for the physical and independent existence with which nature has endowed us. In a word, he must take from man his own powers in order to give him powers that are alien to him and that he can use only with the collaboration of others."[2]

[1] Book I, Chap. VI.
[2] Book II, Chap. VII.

Stripping away all non-essentials, what is sovereign in any society is a will; for sovereignty is the power to decide, and decision is a function of will. In a primary sense, will is the attribute of an individual physical person; but we all conceive of a secondary sense in which it is the attribute of a corporate person. In this secondary sense, the sovereign will is a collective will. A collective will may be said to manifest itself when individual wills are combined to make joint decisions.

What happens, however, when individual wills resist combination, when they conflict?

In that case there must be some agreed device, however arbitrary, for deriving from the conflict of wills what may be represented as a collective will. The device with the widest acceptance in modern societies is that of representing a majority as the whole. In practice, a variety of modifications may be applied: the voting population may be limited, the scope of decision may be restricted, votes may be weighted, pluralities may be accepted in place of true majorities, or a majority of two-thirds may be required. Whatever the qualifications, the device of majority rule in itself, although a pragmatic equivocation, has widespread acceptance. We are so used to it, in fact, that we accept it as if it were nature's norm.

Rousseau appears to adopt a more radical and less equivocal solution to the problem of deriving one will from many. By simply depriving men of their individuality he eliminates all individual wills. When men no longer exist as individuals they no longer have individual interests; when they exist only as members of the body politic their only interest is the interest of all, which is the same for all. Since will tends to accord with interest, the one interest engenders one will. Rousseau calls the one will that results from the elimination of human individuality (and the consequent elimination of individual interests) "the general will."

It is clear, however, that we should not take him so literally.

The total transformation of human nature that he calls for could be accomplished, he says, only by a leader of such extraordinary aptitudes as only a god could possess.[1] The total transformation of human nature is, then, an ideal that he does not expect to be realized. This means that, after the social contract in which all men supposedly surrender their individuality, they will nevertheless exist in two capacities: as recalcitrant individuals, still, with their respective individual interests (which conflict), and as members of the whole, sharing the single interest of the whole. In the one capacity they are many; in the other, one. In the one capacity they represent a multiplicity of wills; in the other, the general will. So the problem of the many or the one remains.

Rousseau falls back, then, on the rule of the majority to reveal the general will, which is sovereign. Unlike the theorists of liberal democracy, however, he does not make the widest agreement among individual wills appear as the will of the whole people. He tries to insure, rather, that the voters shall deliberately cast their votes in their capacity as parts of the collectivity, not in their residual capacity as individuals. To this end, he devises a variety of conditions to define the circumstances in which voting may take place; but he clearly remains unconvinced, himself, of the effectiveness of these conditions in preventing individual interest from being represented in the results. He decides that the state to which his design would be applicable must be neither "too large to be well governed, nor too small to maintain itself alone."[2] (Ancient Sparta, republican Rome, and his native Geneva, with a population of c. 20,000, are the examples he cites.) At another point he says the state must be small enough so that each member may be known by all.[3] Again, the state must be economically self-sufficient. It must enjoy peace and prosperity. At the last he has made so many

[1] Book II, Chap. VII.
[2] Book II, Chap. IX.
[3] Book II, Chap. X.

conditions (some mutually contradictory) that he can cite only
Corsica as a European country fit for the realization of his design.
It is not altogether clear at some points that what he is writing
is not utopian fiction. What is quite clear in the light of subsequent history, which he could not have anticipated, is its
ideological import.

7

Rousseau is never able satisfactorily to resolve the key
question: how to know what the general will is when particular
issues are presented for its decision. His state has a sovereign
with a sovereign will, as every state must; but the sovereign is a
notional person rather than a tangible person. It is invisible, as
God is invisible, and the problem of obeying its will is like the
problem of obeying God's will, that of knowing what it is.
According to widespread belief, God's will is made known
directly only to a single prophet or perhaps to a priesthood. In
the case of the general will the procedure that suggests itself is to
take a vote among the component cells of the notional person
called "the people." However, in such a vote unanimity itself
cannot be relied on, for "there is often a considerable difference
between the will of all and the general will."[1] If all the votes cast
are cast by the voters in their capacity as individuals, rather than

---

[1] Book II, Chap. III. In what one can regard only as intellectual sleight of
hand, not to be taken seriously, Rousseau does add here that the votes which
represent individual interest rather than the general will must always divide
equally on both sides of the question at issue, thereby canceling each other
out and leaving only what does represent the general will, the excess of votes
on one side or the other. If his flat statement to this effect, unaccompanied by
any supporting argument, could be taken seriously, the rule of the majority
would retain its validity. But in that case there could be no such phenomenon
as "the will of all," different from "the general will," for such a will would, by
definition, be unanimous rather than equally divided, as this passage would
have it.

in their capacity as parts of the whole, they do not represent the general will. But even if the voters do cast their votes as parts of the whole, excluding all taint of individual interest and voting only for what they conceive to be the one common interest, their votes may still not represent the general will because they may be honestly mistaken in what they conceive the common interest to be. The general will, by Rousseau's definition, is neither the aggregate of individual wills nor even the consensus of the citizenry on what is in the common interest. The general will is what actually is in the common interest, as distinct from what the voters may mistakenly believe to be in the common interest.

"The general will is always right and always on the side of the public interest."[1] Rousseau calls what is always right and always on the side of the public interest "the general will" because he assumes, not implausibly, that this is what the people as a corporate whole must will if they know what it is. Every person, we suppose, wills what is in his own self-interest, and so we may suppose that the corporate person, too, wills what is in its own self-interest. There are, however, two practical difficulties, as he recognizes, in knowing what is right and in the public interest with respect to any particular issue that may arise for decision. One is the lack of assurance that the votes are not determined by the individual interests of the voters. The other is that the voters, even though uninfluenced by their individual interests, may be honestly mistaken about what is right in terms of the public interest, may out of ignorance vote for what is wrong, in which case what they vote for will not represent the general will, which is represented only by what actually is in the public interest. "The people, left to itself, always wills the good; but, left to itself, it is not always able to recognize it."[2]

Having presented the problem, Rousseau proceeds to provide the solution. Observing that "the general will is always right,

[1] Book II, Chap. III.
[2] Book II, Chap. VI.

but the judgment that guides it is not always enlightened," he adds: "It is necessary to make it see things as they are, sometimes as they must appear to it, to show it the right path which it seeks. . . ."[1]

This raises the question: who is to make the people see things as they are, who is to show which path is right?

"The legislator," Rousseau answers.

8

ANYONE WHO HAS studied the *Social Contract* knows that it contains mutually inconsistent statements and arguments, for Rousseau was straining his ingenuity to provide perfect answers to questions, implicit in the conception of a single sovereign called "the people," for which no perfect answers could be provided. One of these questions arose out of the fact that, even if all the conditions he made for voting were met, the voters might still, out of ignorance, vote for what they believed to be right but was in fact wrong and therefore not in accordance with the general will.

When the question arose, the answer Rousseau gave was that there had to be one man who would guide the people, showing it what the right choice was—that is to say, telling it what the general will was, what the will of the people was. This one man would know what the general will was, even though the people, of itself, did not know what it was. It is this man whom Rousseau calls "the legislator."

---

[1] Book II, Chap. VI. Rousseau is guilty of linguistic confusion here in referring to the general will as a person who seeks the right path but is not always guided by a judgment that is enlightened. He is not the only writer who has, on occasion, confused the subjective and objective senses of the word "will," will as a personal attribute with what is willed. Normally, however, he uses the term "general will" to denote what is willed.

The chapter on the legislator (Book II, Chap. VII) stands alone in the *Social Contract*, as if it had been composed merely to answer an otherwise unanswerable question, thereafter to be forgotten. Moreover, the language of the chapter seems to limit the legislator's role to that of instituting the state, which implies that he might disappear from the scene once this had been done. The reader, however, has to face the fact that, if he did disappear after instituting the state, the question of how to know what the general will was, in the absence of public enlightenment, would presumably arise again. In any case, the conception of a charismatic leader who knows what the general will is, even when the voters do not, has gained a certain significance from the historical experience, since Rousseau's day, of totalitarian states under dictators who, without necessarily consulting the people, have expressed the will of the people in terms regarded as infallible.

Rousseau introduces his chapter on the legislator with the following passage, which concludes the chapter that precedes it.

> Individuals see the good that they reject; the public wills the good that it does not see. All are equally in need of guides. Some must be obliged to conform their wills to their reason; others must be taught to know what they will. Then, from public enlightenment there ensues the union in the social body of understanding and will; from it there ensues the exact concurrence of the parties, and at last the greatest force of the whole. This is what gives rise to the need for a legislator.[1]

It is evident that the first qualification for filling the role of the legislator is knowledge of what is right. This, in itself, puts the incumbent above the level of ordinary mortals, and Rousseau goes so far (in the following opening paragraph of the chapter on the legislator) as to say that he would have to be a god (which raises the unanswered question of where one would recruit him).

To discover the best rules of society that are suitable to

[1] Book II, Chap. VI.

nations, what would be needed would be a superior intelligence who saw all the passions of men without himself being subject to any; who had no rapport with our nature, and yet knew it thoroughly; whose own happiness was independent of us, and who nevertheless was willing to concern himself with ours; who, finally, earning for himself a remote future glory, was able to work in one century and reap the credit in another. It would take gods to provide men with laws.[1]

Rousseau proceeds to make a distinction between the legislator, who institutes the state, and "the prince," who then carries it on. The latter need not have the divine attributes of the former. Montesquieu is cited: "In the birth of societies, it is the leaders of republics who shape the institution, after which it is the institution that shapes the leaders of republics." Allowing for such inconsistency and vagueness as is in the text of Rousseau's essay itself, this citation of Montesquieu could plausibly be regarded as the answer to the question raised above, in the third paragraph of this chapter: how to find out what the general will is (i.e., what is right) after the legislator has left the scene.

The powers of the legislator himself, however, have to be god-like in more than knowledge of what is right. They have to include the power of changing the nature of those who are to compose the society to be instituted. Let me here quote again what I quoted in Chapter 6.

Whoever dares undertake to institute a people must feel himself capable of changing human nature, so to speak, of transforming each individual, who by himself is a perfect and single whole, into part of a greater whole from which he somehow receives his life and his being; he must feel himself capable of altering man's constitution in order to reinforce it, of substituting a partial and moral existence for the physical and independent existence with which nature has endowed us. In a word, he must take from man his own powers in order to give him powers that are alien to him and that he can use only with the collaboration of others.

[1] Book II, Chap. VII.

Another answer to the question posed above, in the third paragraph of this chapter, may be that, when men have been denatured by the removal of what makes them individuals, they will no longer vote as individuals. This, however, would not in itself make them capable of knowing what was right in terms of the common interest. They would still have need of guidance, which might be provided, one supposes, by the "prince" who owed his own formation to the state that the legislator had formed.

9

IN CHAPTER 6 I made a distinction between the liberal tradition, which seeks to accommodate individual diversity, and the totalitarian, which seeks to eliminate it by the imposition of conformity. If one consults the whole of Rousseau's intellectual production, rather than the *Social Contract* only, one cannot say that he preferred totalitarianism to liberalism. Bertrand de Jouvenel, after pointing out that he was given to either-or thinking, has summed the matter up in one sentence: "It is truly an obsession with Rousseau that an end must be made of the conflict by which man is torn, that man must either be given wholly to the state—the theme of the *Social Contract*—or he must be left entirely to himself: the theme of *Émile*".[1]

In the *Social Contract*, then, Rousseau provided an ideal model of society in what was to become the totalitarian tradition. The charismatic leader who presides over that society, having the attributes of a god, decides what the will of the

---

[1] De Jouvenel, p. 93.

people is, while the actual people who constitute the society are allowed no choice but conformity to his decision and consequent obedience to his command.

This lack of choice is what our common sense would call lack of freedom. Rousseau, however, calls it enforced freedom. "Whoever refuses to obey the general will," he writes, "will be constrained to do so by the entire body politic: which means simply that he will be forced to be free."[1] The reasoning here is that every member of the body politic, as such, wills what is right by the test of the common interest. Therefore, to force a member of the body politic to conform to what is right, even against his resistance, is to force him to obey his own true will, although in his ignorance he does not know it is his own true will—and obedience to one's own will is, after all, freedom. When we take account, however, of the fact that the general will is whatever the leader says it is, we see that this reasoning assumes a great deal.

There is here a parallel with the logical device I have elsewhere called nominalism,[2] the device satirized by George Orwell in his novel, *Nineteen Eighty-Four*. In the totalitarian society of the novel the official language is called "Newspeak." The slogans of the state, in that language, are "War Is Peace," "Ignorance Is Strength," "Slavery Is Freedom." The government of the state has a "Ministry of Truth," which is responsible for rewriting history, and a "Ministry of Love" that, in addition to directing the secret police, operates the torture chambers.

In Rousseau's conception, only a leader of divine genius is able to found the state in which men are free, albeit by compulsion, and to determine what the general will is. If one were to object that such genius is not to be found among men, one would have to take account of the fact that Rousseau does offer

[1] Book I, Chap. VII.
[2] Halle, 1965, p. 109.

two examples: Lycurgus, who is credited with founding Sparta, and Calvin, who founded the theocratic state of Geneva. The first example has to be dismissed because, if the legendary Lycurgus ever lived, we know nothing about him as an historical person. Calvin, on the other hand, was real; but what we know about him must make us wonder why Rousseau chose him as an example of the infallible genius under which men enjoy true freedom. Rousseau was not a believing Calvinist who accepted as truth what Calvin preached.[1] Here we must attribute his selection of Calvin as an example to his repeatedly manifested weakness in allowing himself to substitute sentiment for disciplined thinking. He was never a serious enough writer on social problems to quite justify, as such, the seriousness of the countless critiques of his work that have been made since his day, not excluding this one. It has happened more than once that a man has written too casually what, contrary to his expectations at the time of writing, was to be studied by successive generations for centuries after.

Nevertheless, the example of Calvin is apt. It makes no difference that he presented himself as the spokesman for God's will rather than for the general will. Both wills are necessarily right, and neither is directly accessible to ordinary mortals in the present state of humanity. They are therefore interchangeable in the foundation of a totalitarian state. When Calvin established his rule in Geneva, he summoned all the citizens, ten at a time, and required them to subscribe to *Twenty-one Articles of Christian Doctrine* that he and his colleague, Farel, had composed. This document was the equivalent of the "Little Red Book" of Mao Tse-tung's thoughts to which all Chinese today are constrained to subscribe. When a dissenter called Michel Servetus, passing through Geneva, was recognized,

---

[1] At the point where Rousseau cites Calvin, Voltaire wrote in the margin of his copy of the *Social Contract*: "Senseless praise of a vile disputant and absurd priest whom you detest in your heart." De Jouvenel, p. 229.

Calvin's government seized him and had him burned at the stake.[1]

If, then, we are dealing with two opposed political traditions —the liberal tradition which seeks to accommodate diversity and the totalitarian tradition which imposes conformity—Rousseau's choice of Calvin to exemplify the latter is not inappropriate.

Neither Mussolini nor Hitler invoked earlier authority for the totalitarian states they set up, but the correspondence of those states, and of their own roles in instituting them, to the model put forward in the *Social Contract* is striking. Lenin, Mao Tse-tung, and Fidel Castro invoked the authority of Karl Marx for the states they instituted; but we shall see that there is no such correspondence between these states and any model put forward by Marx as there is between them and Rousseau's model.

10

IN EIGHTEENTH-CENTURY Europe a traditional society was still organized on the basis of a doctrine in which thoughtful men had ceased to believe: the doctrine that sovereignty had been vested in princes by God, who had appointed them as his lieutenants to rule over other men. This doctrine had given way, in the course of two centuries, to the doctrine that sovereignty belonged to collective entities called "peoples," rather than to princes. It followed implicitly that the peoples must be freed from a rule that was tyrannical because illegitimate.

---

[1] In a footnote attached by Rousseau to his citation of Calvin, he wrote: "As long as the love of the fatherland and of liberty remain unextinguished among us, the memory of this great man will never cease to be blessed." Let each reader judge for himself Rousseau's use of the word "liberty" in this context.

The men who represented the new legitimacy, however, were not revolutionaries in the sense that the term was to acquire after 1789. They had no plans of action and, to the extent that they thought of bringing about the changes that the doctrine of popular sovereignty implied, what they had before their eyes as a precedent was the English procedure, exemplified in 1688, of bloodless constitutional reform. Even when the Estates General met in Paris on May 5, 1789, no one appears to have had mass violence in mind. The significance of the mob action that brought down the Bastille two months and nine days later was that, by providing a demonstration of effective revolutionary violence, it set a new and more vivid precedent alongside the old.

This precedent was to be reinforced by the dramatic course the French Revolution then took, which has, ever since, made it the model that revolutionaries have had in mind. It is not too much to say that Karl Marx's imagination was entranced by the dream of seeing the drama repeated, albeit with such recasting as was called for by new circumstances.

Even though Voltaire, Montesquieu, the Encyclopedists, and Rousseau represented the doctrine of popular sovereignty, with all its implications for the survival of the rule under which they lived, they were not revolutionaries of a species that, after all, was not to come into being before 1789. They maintained an academic detachment, not going beyond the literary composition of political theory. The *Social Contract* belongs to the category of Plato's *Republic* and More's *Utopia* rather than to that of the *Communist Manifesto*. It concentrates on the design of an ideal society rather than on the destruction of the existing society; and, while the realization of the ideal society would entail the abolition of the existing society, it is clear that Rousseau did not have its realization seriously in mind. Therefore, while the Rousseau of the *Social Contract* may be compared with Hobbes, to attempt a comparison between him and Marx

would be like attempting a comparison between Shakespeare and Napoleon. They belong to different categories.

As de Jouvenel observed, however, there were two Rousseaus. There was the Rousseau of the *Social Contract*, and there was the Jean-Jacques of the two *Discourses*, the *Émile*, and the *Confessions*.[1] Unlike the Rousseau of the *Social Contract*, Jean-Jacques does anticipate, in his attitude, the revolutionaries of the nineteenth and twentieth centuries.

With the advent of Jean-Jacques upon the scene of history we appear to enter the age of romanticism at one bound. He is the first romantic, the precursor of the romanticism of the nineteenth century, and we cannot understand him at all unless we understand him in these terms.

Romanticism embraces a complex of attitudes that is easier to recognize than define. In this it is like a flavor or an odor that is as indescribable as it is familiar. We all know the taste of chocolate, but who could find words to describe it to someone who had never known it? Rather than attempt a comprehensive definition of romanticism, then, I shall begin by citing a prime characteristic which applies conspicuously to Jean-Jacques and is relevant to the political thought that developed after him. That characteristic is introspection, the preoccupation of the romantic individual with his own feelings. The romantic artist tends to be more interested in his inner response to the external world than in that world for its own sake. He cultivates his own sensibilities, and everything he produces tends to be self-consciously autobiographical.

Johann Sebastian Bach was a classical as opposed to a romantic composer, and it occurs to no one to interpret his compositions as autobiographical. The cantatas, the Brandenburg Concertos, the Art of the Fugue, the Musical Offering—none of these can be interpreted as representing a personal *cri de coeur*, as being the composer's revelation of his naked soul confronting

[1] See above, Chap. 9.

a cruel world. On the other hand, commentators agree in interpreting Tschaikowsky's Sixth Symphony, the "Pathétique," as an account of the rebelliousness of his soul, its unhappiness, ending at last in its noble resignation to the tragedy of the artist's life in an unfeeling world.

One can hardly imagine, before the end of the eighteenth century, a poet apostrophizing the west wind in such personal terms as Shelley did:

> I fall upon the thorns of life! I bleed!
> A heavy weight of hours has chained and bowed
> One too like thee: tameless, and swift, and proud.

And ever since Stendhal the heroes of novels have commonly represented the novelist's romanticized image of himself. Norman Mailer's *Armies of the Night* is ostensibly a reporter's account of an anti-war demonstration in Washington, but in fact it is an account of his own inner being confronted by the spectacle of the demonstration. Anatole France's remarkable dictum, "The good critic is the one who recounts the adventures of his soul among masterpieces," applies only to romantic criticism.

The romantic's introspection, generally expressing itself in self-pity, is full-blown in the Jean-Jacques who wrote the *Confessions*, which reveal the adventures of his soul in a wicked world. Contrast him with his contemporary, Voltaire, who in his writing always manifested personal detachment from a world that he regarded, for the most part, with ironic objectivity.

Here is how the *Confessions* begin:

> I undertake that which is without precedent and which, in its execution, will remain without imitation. I wish to display to my kind a man in all the truth of nature; and that man is to be myself. Myself alone. I feel my own heart and I know men. I am not made like any of those I have seen; I make bold to believe that I am not made like any who exist.

He then goes on to say that nature has broken the mold in which

he was cast, so that he is different from anyone who will ever exist, as well as from all who have existed or do still.

In the pages that follow, faithful to his determination to paint his own portrait in all the truth of nature, Jean-Jacques does not refrain from reporting shameful actions on his part, nor does he pretend that they are other than shameful. Nevertheless, as between himself and the world there can be no doubt where his sympathies lie. On the first page of his *Confessions*, still, he pictures himself before the heavenly throne on the Day of Judgment, addressing his Maker: "Eternal being, assemble around me the innumerable host of my kind: let them listen to my confessions, let them lament at my indignities, let them blush at my afflictions."

The romantic polarity between the *myself alone* and *the world* always casts the former in the protagonist's role, the latter in the role of villain. So it is that, in Jean-Jacques, we find the first conspicuous example of the romantic vision in which one's own soul is shown as suffering in a society that is alien to it because it is callous, low-minded, greedy, oppressive, and conspiratorial.

This alienation of the individual from society is basic to the psychology of the revolutionary in the nineteenth and twentieth centuries.

If the Rousseau of the *Social Contract* concludes the lineage of Plato and Hobbes, the Jean-Jacques of the *Confessions* founds a new line, that of the alienated individual.

11

THE INTROSPECTION of the romantic leads to a view of organized society as a monster bent on stifling the natural

nobility that the individual feels within himself. The individual therefore adopts an attitude of defiant alienation.

Rousseau first made his name in 1749 with the publication of his prize-winning "discourse" on the question set by the Academy of Dijon: "whether the revival of the sciences and the arts has contributed to the corruption or the purification of behavior." Up to this time one could have taken for granted the answer, that the sciences and arts had, of course, contributed to the refinement of human behavior. Jean-Jacques, however, coming upon the question in the *Mercure de France*, which he was reading while walking along the road from Paris to Vincennes, experienced a revelation that struck him down like some arrow from the sky. Years later, in a letter to M. de Malesherbes, he told how he fell under a tree by the roadside, where he lay for half an hour in a state of inner turmoil, weeping. "Oh sir," he wrote, "if ever I had been able to set down in writing one quarter of what I saw and felt under that tree, how clearly I would have shown all the contradictions of the social system, with what force I would have exposed all the abuses of our institutions, how simply I would have demonstrated that man is naturally good and that it is only by means of these institutions that men become wicked!"[1]

Here, under these romantic circumstances, was born a conception that would define left-wing radicalism up to our own present. The established society, in this conception, is the enemy.

Hobbes, looking outward upon the scene of the religious wars, saw the propensity of men in a state of nature to destroy one another. He concluded that, simply to save themselves from themselves, they had to place themselves under the rule of that monstrous leviathan called the state. Jean-Jacques, looking inward, saw only the natural nobility of men. Impressed by the antithesis between that nobility and organized society, it was

[1] Rousseau (Jan. 12, 1762), 1959, p. 1134.

easy for him to conceive that not the nature of man but the leviathan itself was the source of evil. For those who came after him the implication would be clear: only get rid of the state and the natural goodness of man will prevail ever after.

From Plato through the Rousseau of the *Social Contract*, political theorists had tended to construct models of society as it might be rather than make plans for the destruction of society as it was. After 1789, however, a new line of political theorists came into being. Preoccupied with the evils of society as it was, they adopted the objective of destroying it. If the question of what should follow was raised, they disposed of it briefly in terms of the revelation that had come to Jean-Jacques on the road to Vincennes: when there was no longer an oppressive political organization to sustain such evils as class privilege and the exploitation of man by man, then men would spontaneously regulate their mutual relations in such a way that there would be no need for the constraints associated with such an organization, therefore no need for any state at all.

The revolutionary profession in which Karl Marx and so many others were to make their careers did not exist as such before 1789. In every generation since, however, it has been adopted by those whose alienation is so deep as to rule out a career within the framework of society as it is.[1] In the course of time it has developed its own professional skills, its own authoritative texts, and its own ethics, A large part of its appeal, for those who have adopted it, has been as a way of life. It is free of the disciplines that other professions impose on their practitioners, such as fixed hours of work and acceptance of routine drudgery. It involves travel, conspiracy, and drama, and it is so open ended in the direction of the future as to accommodate ineffable visions of a worldwide transformation brought about

---

[1] In 1970, making this point in a lecture at the Graduate Institute of International Studies in Geneva, I asked that any student in the audience who was planning a career as a professional revolutionary raise his hand. One student did.

by one's own agency. These are the rewards of a way of life that entails, as well, poverty, insecurity, furtive living, and spells of imprisonment.

Although human motivation is always elusive, one must attribute the widest possible range of motives to those who adopt this modern profession. There is genuine idealism and there is the Pharisaism that imitates it; there is the psychological need to be dedicated to a cause, which is what makes the profession more than a profession, a vocation; there is the appeal of comradeship in the cause, the intoxication of marching in step with others, open hand or clenched fist upraised; there is the satisfaction of having an enemy in the form of a monstrous abstraction to whose image one can attach all the evils of our common life. Finally, there is the appeal of being free to indulge as a virtue the destructive impulse we all know.

I have already remarked that the professional revolutionaries of the nineteenth and twentieth centuries have tended to be wholly preoccupied with the destruction of existing society, so that they have given no thought, or virtually none, to what might come after. An extreme statement of this occurs in one of the series of pamphlets that the anarchists, Michael Bakunin and Sergei Nechaev, wrote in 1869:

> The group that foments the revolution will not try to impose on the people any political organization from above: the organization of the future society will doubtless arise from the people themselves. Our business is simply destruction, terrible, complete, universal and ruthless.[1]

The orthodox Marxists do not differ from the anarchists about the absence, from the world at which they aim, of all such institutions as we identify with the state. Karl Marx concentrated almost exclusively on the destruction of organized society as it was, not concerning himself with the shape of the society that

[1] Quoted from *The Catechism of a Revolutionist* in Wilson, p. 277. Original in Dragomanov, 1896. Other like quotations may be found in Carr, pp. 379–380.

would come into being after the task of destruction had been completed. In all the volumes of his writings there are only a few brief and isolated statements of what the millennial society will be like. Two of these are relevant here. In the *Manifesto of the Communist Party* he wrote that, when "class distinctions have disappeared, and all production has been concentrated in the hands of a vast association of the whole nation, the public power will lose its political character. Political power, properly so called, is merely the organized power of one class for oppressing another."[1]

In *The German Ideology* he wrote that

> ... in the Communist society, where each one does not have a circumscribed sphere of activity but can train himself in any branch he chooses, society by regulating the common production makes it possible for me to do this today and that tomorrow, to hunt in the morning, to fish in the afternoon, to carry on cattle-breeding in the evening, and after supper to engage in criticism —just as I please—without becoming either hunter, fisherman, shepherd, or critic.[2]

Marx's *alter ego*, Friedrich Engels, wrote that when the aims of the Revolution had been accomplished the state would "wither away."[3] Lenin later echoed this statement, adding that no state machinery, "no special instrument of repression," would be needed in the post-Revolutionary society, because "the armed nation itself" would deal with the occasional excesses of individuals "as simply and as readily as any crowd of civilized

---

[1] The quoted passage is to be found near the end of Chap. II. A substantially identical passage occurs in Marx, 1956, p. 197.

Engels was co-author with Marx of the *Manifesto* and a number of other important works. It is generally understood, and Engels said as much, that the major contribution was Marx's. I have therefore adopted throughout these pages, as a matter of convenience, the common custom of referring to Marx only as the author of this and other works written jointly with Engels.

[2] Marx, 1962 i.

[3] Engels, 1959, p. 387.

people, even in modern society, parts a pair of combatants or does not allow a woman to be outraged."[1]

The sufficiency of destruction, then, is fundamental to the conceptual world of the professional revolutionaries who first came into existence after 1789. It is clear that, while the model of the totalitarian societies labeled Marxist today is to be found in the thought of the man who wrote the *Social Contract*, the antecedents of Marx's own Marxism, and of Marxism-Leninism, are to be found in the thought of his polar opposite, the man who wrote the two discourses.[2]

12

ALIENATION and the destructive temper associated with the revolutionaries of the nineteenth and twentieth centuries represent an attitude that first came to prominence with the Jean-Jacques of the two discourses and the *Confessions*. This attitude, however, would hardly have become dominant, as it did, if it had not responded to developing new social circumstances. There were more important factors to support it than the disposition of maladjusted persons (which means most of us) to cultivate romantic visions of themselves, using society as a foil.

Before history reached the watershed that we associate with the French Revolution (if only for convenience), it had been easier for the individual to identify himself with society. In the first place, the society with which he identified himself was generally small. It was the peasant commune, the small town, or the district. Most of those living before the revolution whom we

---

[1] Lenin, 1919, Chap. V, Section 2.
[2] Rousseau's seminal vision was presented in the two discourses he wrote for two successive prize contests organized by the Academy of Dijon. I shall hereafter refer to the two discourses together.

now identify as Frenchmen did not think of themselves as such. If they thought of themselves as belonging to anything larger than their immediate locality, which might be a mountain valley, it would have been to a *pays* like Brittany, Burgundy, or Languedoc. Even Paris, which today has a population of more than three million (excluding its suburbs), still had a population under 550,000 at the time of the Revolution. Before the Revolution there was no French nation at all in the modern sense of the term.[1]

Another factor was that, living close to the soil in an agricultural society, people thought of themselves as depending as much on nature as on social organization. It was the earth, rather than a social system, that fed or failed to feed them in return for their labor. Just as bad weather is not a cause for political protest among us today (although it will become so if we learn to control the weather), so many of the afflictions men suffered in the past, which today might call for political change, were accepted as belonging to the order of nature.

Finally, there was the legitimacy of tradition. The basic conditions under which one generation lived did not differ substantially from those in which its predecessors had lived; so that people were disposed to accept those conditions as if they had always existed and represented God's unchangeable will. Over the generations they had had time to adjust to them, and so they did not seem alien.

The limitations and the stability of the conditions under which people had so long lived were coming to an end in the eighteenth century. Technological developments, which we identify with the industrial revolution, were about to create new means of transportation and communication that would make the small community increasingly obsolete. They were beginning to create new modes of production that, in addition to

---

[1] I make this point more fully, with supporting evidence, in Halle, 1965, Chap. 9.

concentrating populations in great urban centers, would replace their largely natural environment with an increasingly artificial environment to which they had not had time to adapt. These changes, themselves, would break the bonds of tradition, leaving people spiritually and morally adrift in an increasingly alien world. The day was coming when A. E. Housman's Shropshire lad would be speaking for us all when he referred to himself as

> ... a stranger and afraid
> In a world I never made.

What Jean-Jacques did in the two discourses was to provide the increasingly alienated individuals who came after him with the dream of an idyllic world regarded as the natural condition of things, which had preceded the development of the increasingly intolerable institutions against which they stood opposed. In terms of this dream, the destruction of the monstrous leviathan was a sufficient objective. There was no need to design a replacement for it, as political philosophers from Plato to the Rousseau of the *Social Contract* had done.

13

In Chapter 11 I said that the revelation which came to Jean-Jacques on the road to Vincennes would define left-wing radicalism up to our own present. This radicalism, as opposed to that of the right wing, is the primary radicalism of the period since the French Revolution. It is the radicalism of the intellectual communities, of academics, writers, and artists. Right-wing radicalism, typified by movements called fascist, is secondary in that, for the most part, it represents an anti-intellectual reaction against the social disorder and destruction implicit in the

radicalism of the left. As such, it glorifies the state under the guise of patriotism and promotes those elements in it that maintain order by the imposition of discipline from without. Because the confrontation, here, is between intellectuals and anti-intellectuals, left-wing radicalism has an intellectual respectability lacking in right-wing radicalism. It is grounded in generations of profound philosophical thought.

As convenient a beginning as we can find for that thought is in the philosopher whose work came to dominate European philosophical thinking for more than a generation after the French Revolution, Georg Wilhelm Friedrich Hegel (1770–1831).[1]

Philosophy through the centuries before the French Revolution had generally described a static rather than an evolving world. This was possible because, until modern times, secular change was so slow that it could hardly be observed from generation to generation. The basic terms of human life on this planet were quite different at the time of Christ from what they had been ten thousand years before, but they were not different for the generation of the sons from what they had been for the generation of their fathers. Secular change, however, was constantly accelerating, to the point where now, in our own day, middle-aged men find themselves living in a world that has evolved radically since their childhood. It was only about the beginning of the nineteenth century that the pace of secular change reached a point at which it was marked within a single lifetime. The new and increasing awareness of such change, toward the end of the eighteenth century, meant that ontological thinking would have to be in terms of an evolving rather than a static world. Charles Darwin's theory of biological evolution would not be published until 1859, but it was being anticipated long before that, notably in the speculations of his grandfather,

---

[1] Hegel, himself, was neither left wing nor right wing. He was a rationalist, he believed in customary law, and he was a liberal in the sense that he saw social or political history as a desirable progress toward the realization of human freedom.

Erasmus Darwin, whose *Zoonomia* was published in 1794, when Hegel was twenty-four years old.

What preoccupied Hegel was the evolution of human thought, as represented by the history of philosophy, which he saw as a cumulative process in time through which "the Absolute Idea," as he termed it, was being progressively realized. "The Absolute Idea" was synonymous with "God" and with "the rational." Although Hegel never explicitly predicted the future, the implication of his philosophy was teleological. Mankind, in its developing thought, was God realizing himself, was the progressive completion of a rationality that was basic to being.

The process by which this evolution was realized, in Hegel's conception, was dialectical. Any philosophical view that, for its day, becomes dominant among men is bound to be partial and one-sided, in consequence of which it provokes by way of reaction an opposing or alternative view that tends to overcorrect it by going to the other extreme, and so thought is progressively corrected, improved, amplified. It is not hard to foresee a day when this process will be completed, when man will be rounded out in knowledge, when the rational will be fully realized, when the wholeness of God, of man, of the Absolute Idea will have been achieved.[1]

The dynamics of Hegel's philosophy were complemented, then, by a conception, that of partialness, which accorded with the conception of alienation that was to be basic to left-wing radicalism. The fact that God or man was completing himself through the dialectical process meant that he was incomplete, that there was a separation between his partial self and what needed to be assimilated by it in order to complete it. One way of putting this would be to say that the objective world was alienated from man's subjective self. The history of human

---

[1] "God is only God insofar as he knows himself; his knowing himself is, furthermore, a self-consciousness in man and man's knowledge *of* God that goes on to man's knowing himself *in* God." Hegel, 1970, Paragraph 564, p. 374, translated in Kaufmann, 1966, p. 275.

thought was the history of man overcoming alienation by progressively comprehending the objective world.

Not only were the concepts of evolution and alienation appropriate to the times in which Hegel wrote, the emphasis on the progressive acquisition of knowledge was no less appropriate. The great age of the expansion of human knowledge had begun, and the technological application of the new knowledge was giving mankind increasing mastery over its environment. Newtonian mechanics were being followed by those sensational discoveries relating to electricity and magnetism that, while in themselves reducing the alien character of the external world, would also give mankind increasing power over it. The Hegelian mythology was not, after all, without correspondence to experience.

In the first half of the nineteenth century, Continental philosophy was under the spell of Hegel's thought. The dualism of a world broken in two was accepted, and with it man's mission to mend the break, to achieve wholeness. Hegel, himself, was given the chair of philosophy at the University of Berlin in 1818, the year in which Karl Marx was born. He continued as professor there until his death in 1831. Four years later, Karl Marx entered the university as a doctoral candidate in philosophy, and the philosophy he studied there for the next five years was all Hegelianized philosophy, philosophy presented in the conceptual framework created by Professor Hegel.

14

THE PROFESSIONAL revolutionaries of the nineteenth century congregated in the cafés of Geneva, Zürich, Brussels, and Paris, and in the rooming houses of London. As is the case with

any group of intellectuals, only an occasional individual among them had an original mind of his own. In this respect, Karl Marx towered above the others.

Few of the others, moreover, came from a background as cultivated and cosmopolitan as his. The fact that his native Rhineland had been under the rule of Napoleonic France until three years before his birth contributed to the cosmopolitanism it would have derived anyway from its proximity to the countries on the western fringe of Europe. Its direct exposure to the intellectual radiation of the French Revolution had made it the least illiberal of the territories that, after 1815, came under the reactionary rule of Prussia.

In the home town of Trier, Marx's father was a prosperous lawyer whose intellectual pastime was the study of seventeenth-century French poetry. He was the scion of a long line of rabbis, but the French Englightenment, on which he had fed, had caused him to abandon the Jewish religion to which he had been brought up. When the Prussian government imposed anti-Semitic legislation that would have barred him from the practice of his profession, he changed his name from Hirschel to Heinrich and joined the Evangelical Church. This had its influence on his son Karl, if we may suppose that the explicit anti-Semitism he was to manifest all his life represented an impulse that he would not have felt if it had not been possible to mistake him for a Jew. In a polemical essay written in 1843, *On the Jewish Question*, he associated Judaism with the sinister power of money, so that his defenders in a later age have had some color for saying that, in the unbridled denunciations of the Jews it contains, the real object of his attack was not the Jews as such. This would still not make the denunciations complimentary to the Jews as such.

Even though the revolutionaries believed in human equality, they were human, and it may be that Karl Marx's prestige among them did not suffer from his wife's aristocratic lineage.

The descendent of rabbis had married the daughter of Baron Johann Ludwig von Westphalen, whose Scottish mother was descended from the earls of Argyll and the earls of Angus. Above all, Marx was an educated man with a doctorate in philosophy and a thorough grounding in the classics of European literature. This must have given him the advantage that the educated always have over the relatively uneducated when it came to arguing with his fellow revolutionaries. It must also have contributed to the self-confidence he never lacked.

Marx's mind belonged to literature more than to any form of science. All his life he was addicted to dramatic literature in particular, and his thought was directed by a powerful dramatic imagination. It is significant that his two favorite authors, whom he is said to have known in large part by memory, were Aeschylus and Shakespeare. The affinity with Aeschylus is especially understandable, for *Prometheus Bound* represents, as no other work does, the scale and temper of Marx's mind.

One of the elements that Marx's intellectual background contributed to the formation of his mind was the conception, so prominent in Western thought from Napoleon to Hitler, of the exceptional individual who, as such, is not bound by the ethical standards that apply to the behavior of ordinary men. Hegel had written about "world-historical individuals," Nietzsche was to write about the "superman" (*Übermensch*), and while each used these respective terms in an intelligent and responsible sense, others would use them in an altogether different sense to justify Caesarism. The conception, in its irresponsible development, is represented by Raskolnikov, the protagonist of Dostoyevsky's *Crime and Punishment*, who murders an old woman to prove himself a great man, superior to the morality of the herd. Describing the theme of an article he has written, he says:

> ... an "extraordinary man" has the right ... to decide in his own conscience to overstep ... certain obstacles. ... Newton

would have had the right, would indeed have been in duty
bound . . . to *eliminate* the dozen or the hundred men for the sake
of making his discoveries known to the whole of humanity. . . .
Lycurgus, Solon, Mahomet, Napoleon . . . all great men . . .
must from their very nature be criminals . . . to remain in the
common rut is what they cannot submit to . . . and to my mind
they ought not, indeed, to submit to it.[1]

The denigration of common ethical standards implicit in this
conception could easily take the form of the romantic Mephistophelianism, of which there are suggestions in Goethe's *Faust*. In
a poetic tragedy called *Oulanem*, which the young Marx left
unfinished, a soliloquy of the eponymous hero contains the
following typical lines:

Now there emerges a man, two legs and a heart,
Who has the power to utter living curses.
Ha, I must bind myself to a wheel of flame
And dance with joy in the circle of eternity!
If there is a Something which devours,
I'll leap within it, though I bring the world to ruins—
The world which bulks between me and the abyss
I will smash to pieces with my enduring curses.[2]

One who began his own writing career young has reason to
appreciate the propriety of viewing with indulgence the youth-
ful attempts of others. We must not make too much of the romantic Mephistophelianism that is so prominent in the lyric and
dramatic poetry of the young Marx. Nevertheless, it does reveal
that the destructive impulse common to us all was especially
strong in him. It was, indeed, represented in his mature self by
the anticipation of a coming revolution that would fill the world
with blood.

Perhaps the young Marx, driven by apocalyptic visions, could
not in any case have settled down to a career as a philosopher or
journalist within the established society. Since, as it transpired,

---

[1] Dostoyevsky, Chap. V.
[2] Marx, 1929, pp. 68–69. Translation from Payne, p. 71.

neither an academic nor a journalistic career was open to one of such independent mind under the Prussian rule of the day, he was virtually driven to choose exile and the career of a professional revolutionary. By 1843, twenty-five years old and newly married, he was already in Paris and embarked on his career.

What most distinguished the Paris of the time was that it was the scene of the French Revolution, which many of its inhabitants could still remember. It seemed likely, as well, to be the scene of a second revolution that was approaching. This second revolution would be the final "world revolution," the proclamation of which was to be composed some four years later by Marx and his friend Engels as the *Manifesto of the Communist Party*. Writing in the summer of 1842, Heinrich Heine gave an account of what it would be like:

> In the second act we see the European and the World Revolution, the great duel between the destitute and the aristocracy of wealth. . . . Wild, gloomy times are roaring toward us, and the prophet who wished to write the new Apocalypse would have to invent entirely new beasts and they would be so terrible that the ancient animal symbols of St. John would be like gentle doves and cupids.[1]

The extent to which the second revolution, in Communist belief, has always been the equivalent of the second coming in Christian belief should not go unnoted. Marx, himself, made the comparison in a passage, later deleted, from *The German Ideology*, writing that the Pope "will be greatly surprised when the Day of Judgement overtakes him . . . —the day when the reflection of burning cities is seen in the heavens, marking the coming of dawn, and when the 'celestial harmonies' consist of the melodies of the 'Marseillaise' and the 'Carmagnole' to an accompaniment of thundering cannon blasting his ears, while

[1] Heine, p. 235. Translation from Payne, p. 103. (I have changed his "wishes" to "wished".)

the guillotine beats time, and the maddened masses scream '*Ça
ira, ça ira,*' . . ."[1]

15

MARX WAS a philosopher only secondarily, and a revolutionist only secondarily. Primarily he was a dramatist, like Aeschylus. He composed his drama of the revolution on the mythic
framework of Hegel's philosophy as Aeschylus had composed
the drama of Prometheus on the framework of Greek myth, and
he was a revolutionary merely in trying to achieve its production.

In Hegel's vision, the world lay broken into two parts: one
was man in his incomplete subjective being, the other the objective external world that was alienated from him. In Marx's
original conception—the philosophical Marxism that preceded
the canonical Marxism of the *Manifesto*—man was a creator who
existed to produce objects of art as a queen bee exists to lay
eggs. The element of greed in his nature, however, moved him
to alienate his creations by selling them for money. (It was as if
a man, unable to resist the lure of gold, should sell his daughter
into prostitution: he would thus be alienating a piece of himself,
making himself more incomplete.) This cumulative process of
alienation ends, however, with the coming of the revolution,
which is equivalent to the second coming in the New Testament,
just as alienation itself is equivalent to the fall of man in the Old
Testament. The revolution ushers in a transitional period of
purgatorial horror, equivalent to that described in Revelation 20,
which foretells how, at the time of the resurrection, Satan will be
turned loose for a spell to spread destruction and suffering
among the nations. All ends, however, with the final regenera-

[1] Marx, 1962, pp. 70–71. Translation from Payne, p. 128.

tion and transfiguration of man, the restoration of his perfection in all its integrity, as it was before the fall. ("For now we know in part," said St. Paul, "and we prophesy in part; but when that which is perfect is come, then that which is in part shall be done away.")

The way the mythic or dreamlike contents of Marx's mind always fell into the basic Hegelian pattern is revealed in the tales he invented about a character called Hans Röckle to amuse his little daughter, Eleanor. In her reminiscences of her father she later wrote:

> Hans Röckle himself was a Hoffman-like magician, who kept a toyshop, and who was always "hard up." His shop was full of the most wonderful things—of wooden men and women, giants and dwarfs, kings and queens, workmen and masters, animals and birds as numerous as Noah got into the Ark, tables and chairs, carriages, boxes of all sorts and sizes. And though he was a magician, Hans could never meet his obligations either to the devil or the butcher, and was therefore—much against the grain —constantly obliged to sell his toys to the devil. Those then went through wonderful adventures—always ending in a return to Hans Röckle's shop.[1]

Not only does Hans Röckle represent man as a creative artist; it is hard to doubt that he represents the particular creative artist who was Karl Marx. It was precisely because Marx was a person of vast and frustrated creativity that, judging others by himself, his conception of man in the abstract was of a frustrated creator.

How does the philosophical Marxism contained in the so-called "Economic and Philosophical Manuscripts of 1844" differ from the canonical Marxism that was born in 1848 with the publication of the *Manifesto*?

The protagonist of philosophical Marxism was a single abstraction called "man," as distinct from the many individual

---

[1] *Karl Marx: A Few Stray Notes*, by Eleanor Marx-Aveling, in Fromm, p. 251.

men of tangible reality. Marx repeatedly referred to this protagonist as a "species being "(*Gattungswesen*). The "species being" is riven by inner conflict. On the one hand, there is the creative side of his nature, which moves him, like Hans Röckle, to produce all sorts of objects of art. On the other, there is the greedy beast within him, which drives him to alienate these works for money. It was surely Marx's dramatic instinct that prompted him to adopt the simple device by which the Marxism of the philosophical manuscripts became the Marxism of the *Manifesto*. In place of the inwardly divided species being, man, he put two characters: the proletarian and the capitalist. The proletarian represented creativity, the capitalist greed. What had been an inner conflict thus became a mortal combat between two characters who stood, respectively, for good and evil.

Where the drama of inner conflict was too sophisticated for popular appreciation, the contest between the good proletarian and the wicked capitalist conformed to the childlike mind that feeds on such fairy tales as "'Jack the Giant-killer" or "Cinderella and her Wicked Sisters," on such comic strips as "Steve Canyon" or "Buzz Sawyer," on stories of the good cowboys and the bad Indians, or the cops and the robbers, or the Rover Boys and the cattle rustlers. By a single transformation, what had begun in Hegelian terms was finally reduced to the simplest level of the common understanding.

At the outset of the new drama that Marx (with his collaborator, Engels) presented in 1848, the wicked capitalist is holding the proletarian in bondage, forcing him to produce to his capacity and under increasingly intolerable conditions, but taking his production away from him and selling it for his own enrichment. As time passes, however, the proletarian is growing in his strength and his anger, while the capitalist, anticipating his own doom, is becoming increasingly fearful and desperate. It is evident that, in the language of the Negro spiritual, "There's a great day coming and it's not far off."

The loss of intellectual sophistication that Marxism suffered, when it underwent the transformation from its philosophical to its canonical form, was the price paid for the popular appeal it has had ever since.

16

IT IS NOT necessarily derogatory of Marx to say that his mind was characterized by its massive simplicity. Such simplicity, in varying degree, characterizes all creative minds, for intellectual creation consists in reducing the complications of the existential chaos to the simplicity of some coherent order. The analytical mind complicates by taking things apart; the creative mind simplifies by putting things together. This is not to say, however, that simplification, in particular instances, cannot go too far.

A related characteristic of Marx's mind was its absoluteness. He was always absolute in his conviction that whatever conception he was expounding represented absolute truth. In this he was more like an Old Testament prophet than like any of the social philosophers from Plato to de Tocqueville. Here one may observe that the prophets move the world more than do the social philosophers.

Between 1844 and 1848 it came to Marx that there was no such thing as the species being, man. The only reality was that of social class. In the *Manifesto*, disregarding his own absoluteness of a few years earlier, he was sarcastic about the Hegelian philosophical disposition of the German socialists who, failing "to express the struggle of one class with the other," thought of themselves as representing "not true requirements, but the requirements of Truth, not the interests of the proletariat, but

the interests of Human Nature, of Man in general, who belongs to no class, has no reality, who exists only in the misty realm of philosophical phantasy." The reality, for Marx, had now become two corporate persons in place of one.[1]

The whole of the Marxism that has moved the world is contained in the relatively few pages of the *Manifesto*. It was written in a few weeks, by contrast with *Capital*, to which he devoted the last three or four decades of his life without finishing it. *Capital*, however, is an economic treatise rather than scripture.

In 1847, when it seemed that the day of the second revolution was almost at hand, various revolutionary organizations made their preparations to assume the leadership. In London something called "The League of the Just" changed its name to "The Communist League" and, at a congress that met in late November, asked Marx to draw up a program, which was to be ready by the beginning of January 1848. During the subsequent weeks in Brussels, where he was living, he seems to have become blocked in his mind about the form and content of the document he had undertaken to write. His hand was forced, at last, by a third-person letter of January 26 from the Central Committee warning him "that if the Manifesto of the C. Party, which he agreed to draw up at the last Congress, does not arrive in London before Tuesday, February 1, further measures will be taken against him."[2] That gave him perhaps three days to finish off the job. The internal evidence of the final product suggests that he finished it off any whichway to meet the deadline. As a literary whole it is grotesque, like a Greek temple

---

[1] It should be noted that a social class is a conceptual abstraction just as a species is. But the species exists as a matter of nature and is unambiguously definable in the case of modern man, so that there is never any question of whether a particular individual organism is or is not a man. It has never been possible, however, to devise a definition of "proletarian" or "bourgeois" that did not leave a wide range of uncertainty about who belonged and who did not. The blood of a man can be distinguished from the blood of a chimpanzee, but not the blood of a proletarian from the blood of a bourgeois. For those of us who prefer peace to the sword, as well as for those of us who prefer reality to fiction, there is much to be said for regarding mankind as one.

[2] Quoted by Payne, p. 162.

hastily completed by some temporary tenement housing. It begins with a half-page introduction that must be classified as bombast. Then, after a first chapter in the language of thought and scholarship, comes a second, full of polemical flourishes, followed by a third in which a variety of schools of socialism with which the author does not agree are denounced and ridiculed. The whole is an incongruous association that embraces a lofty vision of history presented in quiet and magisterial tones, shrill polemics, and petty bickering. The vision of history is what gives it the greatness it has, and the exposition of this vision is in the first chapter.

17

"THE HISTORY of all hitherto existing society is the history of class struggles." This is an admirable opening sentence in its grandeur and simplicity. Its character is maintained in what follows:

> Freeman and slave, patrician and plebeian, lord and serf, guild-master and journeyman, in a word, oppressor and oppressed, stood in constant opposition to one another, carried on uninterrupted, now hidden, now open fight, a fight that each time ended, either in a revolutionary re-constitution of society at large, or in the common ruin of the contending classes.
>
> In the earlier epochs of history we find almost everywhere a complicated arrangement of society into various orders, a manifold gradation of social rank. In ancient Rome we have patricians, knights, plebeians, slaves; in the middle ages feudal lords, vassals, guild-masters, journeymen, apprentices, serfs; in almost all of these classes, again, subordinate gradations.
>
> The modern bourgeois society, that has sprouted from the ruins of feudal society, has not done away with class antagonisms.

It has but established new classes, new conditions of oppression, new forms of struggle in place of the old ones.

Our epoch, the epoch of the bourgeoisie, possesses, however, this distinctive feature; it has simplified the class antagonisms. Society as a whole is more and more splitting up into two great hostile camps, into two great classes directly facing each other: Bourgeoisie and Proletariat.

In these few lines the stage is set for the approaching climax of all history. We see the operation over the millennia of a universal movement that, in its inexorable progress, has at last reduced an original complexity to the polar confrontation of just two contestants over the wide world.

In what follows, Marx fills the outline he has sketched with supporting information that gives the vision verisimilitude and the authority of scholarship. "The discovery of America, the rounding of the Cape, opened up fresh grounds for the rising bourgeoisie." Again:

Modern industry has established the world market, for which the discovery of America paved the way. This market has given an immense development to commerce, to navigation, to communication by land, This development has, in its turn, reacted on the extension of industry; and in proportion as industry, commerce, navigation, railways extended, in the same proportion the bourgeoisie developed, increased its capital, and pushed into the background every class handed down from the Middle Ages.

The reader is captivated because, seeing through Marx's eyes, he feels himself sharing vision with a god. Sentence after sentence brings what seems to be new illumination—for example: "The executive of the modern State is but a committee for managing the common affairs of the whole bourgeoisie." Government will never again look the same to the reader.

The bourgeoisie is first presented as a giant unmatched in his creative energy. But the giant is cold-blooded.

[The bourgeoisie] has pitilessly torn asunder the motley feudal

ties that bound man to his "natural superiors," and has left no other nexus between man and man than naked self-interest, than callous "cash payment." . . . In one word, for exploitation, veiled by religious and political illusions, it has substituted naked, shameless, direct, brutal exploitation. . . . [It] has torn away from the family its sentimental veil, and has reduced the family relation to a mere money relation.

What immediately follows has the same effect as Mark Antony's funeral speech in Act III, Scene ii, of Shakespeare's *Julius Caesar*. Antony, working the mob up to a fury of hatred and vengeance against Caesar's murderers, Brutus and the others, contrives to have their fury build up the more by holding it back at first with his insistence that "Brutus is an honorable man; so are they all, all honorable men." In the same way, Marx now insists on the great accomplishments of the bourgeoisie in the past. "It has accomplished wonders far surpassing Egyptian pyramids, Roman aqueducts, and Gothic cathedrals; it has conducted expeditions that put in the shade all former Exoduses of nations and crusades."

The modern bourgeoisie, however, "is like a sorcerer, who is no longer able to control the powers of the nether world whom he has called up by his spells." Here Marx casts the bourgeoisie in the role of Faust, who paid for his day of godlike supremacy by at last becoming the corrupted minion of Mephistopheles. At last the bourgeoisie sinks to such depths of degradation that "our bourgeois, not content with having the wives and daughters of their proletarians at their disposal, not to speak of common prostitutes, take the greatest pleasure in seducing each others' wives." A reader can see that his wife or his daughter is no longer safe from the monster.

However, "the weapons with which the bourgeoisie felled feudalism to the ground are now turned against the bourgeoisie itself." And, "not only has the bourgeoisie forged the weapons that bring death to itself; it has also called into existence the men who are to wield those weapons—the modern working-

class—the proletarians." At this point the hero enters upon the scene.

"Not only are [the proletarians] the slaves of the bourgeois class and of the bourgeois state, they are daily and hourly enslaved by the machine, by the overlooker [the overseer], and, above all, by the individual bourgeois manufacturer himself."

> ... the cost of production of a workman is restricted almost entirely to the means of subsistence that he requires for his maintenance, and for the propagation of his race. But the price of a commodity, and also of labor, is equal to its cost of production. In proportion, therefore, as the repulsiveness of the work increases the wage decreases. Nay more, in proportion as the use of machinery and division of labor increases, in the same proportion the burden of toil increases, whether by prolongation of the working hours, by increase of the work enacted in a given time, or by increased speed of the machinery, etc.

"The modern laborer," Marx writes, ". . . instead of rising with the progress of industry, sinks deeper and deeper below the conditions of existence of his own class. He becomes a pauper, and pauperism develops more rapidly than population and wealth."

As the misery of the proletarians increases, however, so do their numbers. And as their misery and their numbers increase, so do their class-consciousness and resentment against the bourgeoisie.

> ... with the development of industry the proletariat not only increases in number; it becomes concentrated in greater masses, its strength grows and it feels that strength more. The various interests and conditions of life within the ranks of the proletariat are more and more equalized, in proportion as machinery obliterates all distinctions of labor, and nearly everywhere reduces wages to the same low level. The growing competition among the bourgeois, and the resulting commercial crisis, make the wages of the workers even more fluctuating. The unceasing improvement of machinery, ever more rapidly developing, makes their livelihood more and more precarious;

the collisions between individual workmen and individual bourgeois take more and more the character of collisions between two classes.

The increasing union of the workers

... is helped on by the improved means of communication that are created by modern industry, and that places the workers of different localities in contact with one another. It was just this contact that was needed to centralize the numerous local struggles, all of the same character, into one national struggle between classes. But every class struggle is a political struggle. And that union, to attain which the burghers of the Middle Ages with their miserable highways, required centuries, the modern proletarians, thanks to railways, achieve in a few years.

The final revolution of human history, which is to be made by the proletariat, differs from all the preceding revolutions through which a succession of classes have risen to dominance by the fact that the proletariat, when it rises up, will have become "the immense majority" of the population, and by the fact that its revolutionary mission will be more destructive.

All the preceding classes that got the upper hand sought to fortify their already acquired status by subjecting society at large to their conditions of appropriation. The proletarians cannot become masters of the productive forces of society, except by abolishing their own previous mode of appropriation, and thereby also every other previous mode of appropriation. They have nothing of their own to secure and to fortify; their mission is to destroy all previous securities for and insurances of individual property.

All previous historical movements were movements of minorities, or in the interest of minorities. The proletarian movement is the self-conscious, independent movement of the immense majority. The proletariat, the lowest stratum of our present society, cannot stir, cannot raise itself up without the whole superincumbent strata of official society being sprung into the air.

Marx, in his account of the course of history, stops at the

culminating moment when the Revolution is about to take place. See how, in the last sentence above, "the whole superincumbent strata of official society" are not actually "sprung into the air"— it merely seems certain that they are about to be "sprung into the air." In the next sentence Marx returns to the pre-revolutionary period, resuming and expanding on what he has already written. The nearest he will again come, in the *Manifesto*, to proclaiming the revolution in so many words will be in the conclusion of Chapter I: "What the bourgeoisie ... produces, above all, are its own grave diggers. Its fall and the victory of the proletariat are equally inevitable."

18

THE READER WILL recall from Chapter 15 that, in the philosophical Marxism which preceded the canonical Marxism of the *Manifesto*, the revolution would usher in a transitional period of purgatorial horror. The initial "crude communism" (to use the language of the manuscripts of 1844)

> ... aims to destroy everything which is incapable of being possessed by everyone as private property. It wishes to eliminate talent [which is incapable of being possessed by everyone], etc. by *force*. Immediate physical possession seems to it the unique goal of life and existence. ... The relation of private property remains the relation of the community to the world of things. Finally, this tendency to oppose general private property to private property is expressed in an animal form; *marriage* (which is incontestably a form of *exclusive private property*) is contrasted with the community of women, in which women become communal and common property. ... Just as women are to pass from marriage to universal prostitution, so the whole world of wealth (i.e., the objective being of man) is to pass from the relation of exclusive marriage with the private owner to the

relation of universal prostitution with the community. . . . Universal *envy* setting itself up as a power is only a camouflaged form of cupidity which re-establishes itself and satisfies itself in a different way. . . . Crude communism is only the culmination of such envy and levelling-down on the basis of a *preconceived minimum*. . . . In the relationship with *woman*, as the prey and the handmaid of communal lust, is expressed the infinite degradation in which man exists for himself. . .[1]

At last, however, this "crude communism" develops into the final and true communism, which is "the return of man himself as a *social*, i.e., really human, being, a complete and conscious return which assimilates all the wealth of previous development." If the reader finds this vague as a description of the ultimate human society, what remains of the account will do little to make it clearer:

> Communism as a fully developed naturalism is humanism and as a fully developed humanism is naturalism. It is the *definitive* resolution of the antagonism between man and nature, and between man and man. It is the true solution of the conflict between existence and essence, between objectification and self-affirmation, between freedom and necessity, between individual and species. It is the solution of the riddle of history and knows itself to be this solution.[2]

Thomas Hobbes, one suspects, would not have found this satisfactory as a description of the best possible society under earthly conditions. The language of philosophical discourse suffered a degeneration between the seventeenth and the nineteenth century.

In philosophical Marxism, the vision is of a revolution followed, as the second coming was to be followed, by a period of purgatorial horror that would usher in the kingdom of heaven on earth. The sequence of developments is the same in

---

[1] Marx, 1932, pp. 111–113. Translation from Bottomore, pp. 153–154.
[2] Marx, 1932, p. 144. Translation from Bottomore, p. 155.

the canonical Marxism that represents the ultimate development of the philosophical Marxism. "Between the capitalist and the Communist society," Marx would write in 1875, "lies the period of the revolutionary transformation of the one into the other. To this corresponds a political transition period in which the state can be nothing else but *the revolutionary dictatorship of the proletariat.*"[1]

Toward the end of the second chapter of the *Manifesto* Marx offered an account of this transition period which is worth quoting at length:

> We have seen above that the first step in the revolution by the working class is to raise the proletariat to the position of ruling class, to win the battle of democracy.
>
> The proletariat will use its political supremacy to wrest, by degrees, all capital from the bourgeoisie, to centralize all instruments of production in the hands of the State, i.e., of the proletariat organized as a ruling class; and to increase the total productive forces as rapidly as possible.
>
> Of course, in the beginning, this cannot be effected except by means of despotic inroads on the rights of property, and on the conditions of bourgeois production; by means of measures, therefore, which appear economically insufficient and untenable, but which in the course of the movement outstrip themselves, necessitate further inroads upon the old social order, and are unavoidable as a means of entirely revolutionizing the mode of production. . . .
>
> When, in the course of development, class distinctions have disappeared, and all production has been concentrated in the hands of a vast association of the whole nation, the public power will lose its political character. [This is what Engels and, after him, Lenin would refer to as "the withering away of the State."] Political power, properly so called, is merely the organized power of one class for oppressing another. If the proletariat during its contest with the bourgeoisie is compelled, by the force of circumstances, to organize itself as a class, if, by means of a revolution, it makes itself the ruling class, and, as such, sweeps away by force the old conditions of production, then it will, along with

[1] Marx, 1962 ii, p. 28. Translation from Eastman, p. 355.

these conditions, have swept away the conditions for the existence of class antagonism, and of classes generally, and will thereby have abolished its own supremacy as a class.

In place of the old bourgeois society, with its classes and class antagonisms, we shall have an association in which the free development of each is the condition for the free development of all.[1]

In 1875, in his *Criticism of the Gotha Program,* Marx gave one of his few specific indications of what the ultimate communist society would be like, writing that it would "inscribe upon its banner: 'From each according to his abilities, to each according to his needs!' "[2]

At this point I sum up Marx's vision of the society to come. The proletariat, having become "the immense majority" of the population, will overthrow bourgeois society by a cataclysmic revolution. It will then, for a transitional period, constitute itself the ruling class, maintaining its own dictatorship for the purpose of eliminating the bourgeoisie, centralizing all instruments of production in the hands of the state, and increasing the total productive forces of society. As this is accomplished, society will automatically become classless, the state will automatically wither away, and a permanent condition will be attained in which "the free development of each is the condition for the free development of all." There will then be perfect freedom, not in the sense Rousseau gave the term in the *Social Contract,* but in its common sense. Every individual will be free "to do this today and that tomorrow, to hunt in the morning, to fish in the afternoon, to carry on cattle-breeding in the evening, and after supper to engage in criticism."

[1] Between the third and fourth paragraphs quoted here Marx did list ten measures such as might have to be taken by the proletarian dictatorship. However, in the joint preface to the German edition of 1872, Marx and Engels dismissed this list as being "in some details . . . antiquated." It contains some measures of state despotism, some measures that all liberal democracies have since adopted, and some that would hardly be regarded as practicable today.
[2] Marx, 1962 ii, p. 21. Translation from Eastman, p. 7.

19

In *The State and Revolution*, a gloss on the canonical writings that has itself become canonical, Lenin wrote: "We do not at all disagree with the Anarchists on the question of the abolition of the State as a *final aim*."[1]

The Marxist conception, like the anarchist, was in fundamental accord with the revelation that came to Rousseau on the road to Vincennes, the revelation "that it is only by means of [our] institutions that men become wicked." The form this took in Lenin's formulation was that, "freed from capitalist slavery, from the innumerable horrors, savagery, absurdities and infamies of capitalist exploitation, people will gradually become accustomed to the observation of the elementary rules of social life, known for centuries, repeated for thousands of years in all sermons. They will become accustomed to their observance without force, without constraint, without subjection, without the *special apparatus* for compulsion which is called the State."[2]

Anarchists and Marxists were both followers of Jean-Jacques in the belief that evildoing is not intrinsic to human nature but is, rather, a consequence of social institutions. The difference between them was that the anarchists, closer to Jean-Jacques in this, held that the simple destruction of all political institutions would be automatically followed by the reign of virtue and peace, while the Marxists held that customary human behavior would have to undergo a gradual and far-reaching transformation before political institutions became wholly unnecessary, and that this transformation of human behavior would

[1] Chap. IV, Section 2.
[2] Ibid., Chap. V, Section 2.

automatically entail "the withering away" of political institutions. Where the anarchists saw the enhancement of human behavior as consequent upon the disappearance of the state, the Marxists saw the disappearance of the state as consequent upon the enhancement of human behavior that would follow the end of the class struggle. Since, in the Marxist vision, the enhancement of human behavior could only be gradual, they foresaw a transitional period between the rule of the bourgeoisie and the stateless society. That transitional period was to begin with the revolution, a cataclysmic event soon over, and to be continued under a "dictatorship of the proletariat" throughout the whole course of which the state would be automatically withering away.

Marx, Engels, and Lenin all insisted that the revolution must be bloody and cruel. They appear to have seen a danger that it would fail because, at the last moment, humanitarian feelings would cause those who made it to recoil from absolute ruthlessness. When, however, we trace this insistence on blood and pain back to the young Marx, it becomes hard to doubt that it has deep psychological roots in what I may call the dark side of romanticism. There will be a *Walpurgisnacht* during which women will be common property and all the civilized restraints on behavior will be lifted. Psychic frustrations will then be released, and unholy appetites will be satisfied.

Having made the revolution, the proletariat would then establish its dictatorship. "The proletariat" being, like "the people," a nominal and conceptual person, rather than a visible person, the question arises of how it could exercise a dictatorship, just as the question arose for us earlier (Chap. 5) of how "the people" could exercise sovereignty. The French socialist, Charles Péguy, gave this question a practical formulation in 1900, when he said: "I should like to know who will actually be the persons who will exercise the dictatorship of the proletariat."[1]

---

[1] Cited by Wolfe, p. 238.

In *The State and Revolution* Lenin referred to the dictatorship of the proletariat as "the discharge of all the functions of Government by the majority of the population and by every individual of the population." To this he added:

> Capitalist culture has created industry on a large scale in the shape of factories, railways, posts, telephones and so forth: and on this basis the great majority of functions of "the old State" have become enormously simplified and reduced, in practice, to very simple operations such as registration, filing and checking. Hence they will be quite within the reach of any literate person...

Again:

> We have but to overthrow the capitalists, to crush with the iron hand of the armed workers the resistance of these exploiters, to break the bureaucratic machine of the modern State—and we have before us a highly technically-fashioned machine freed of its parasites, which can quite well be set going by the united workers themselves, hiring their own technical advisers, their own inspectors, their own clerks. . . .[1]

The whole of this activity, he added, was to be "under the management of the armed proletariat."[2] This last statement throws us back upon the original question. But once again:

> The exploiters are unable, of course, to suppress the people without a most complex machine for performing this duty; but *the people* can suppress the exploiters even with a very simple "machine"—almost without any "machine" at all, without any special apparatus—by the simple *organization of the armed masses* (such as the Councils of Workers' and Soldiers' Deputies. . .).[3]

Although Lenin foresaw that there would have to be officials, their control by "the people" would be assured, "without exception, by the unreserved application of the principle of election and, *at any time*, re-call; and the approximation of their salaries to 'the ordinary pay of the workers.' . . ."[4] Finally:

> When all have learned to manage, and really do manage, social-

[1] Chap. III, Section 2.
[2] Chap. III, Section 3.
[3] Chap. V, Section 2.
[4] Chap. III, Section 2.

ized production, when all really do keep account and control of the idlers, gentlefolk, swindlers, and suchlike "guardians of capitalist traditions," the escape from such general registration and control will inevitably become so increasingly difficult, so much the exception, and will probably be accompanied by such swift and severe punishment (for the armed workers are very practical people, not sentimental intellectuals, and they will scarcely allow anyone to trifle with them), that very soon the necessity of observing the simple, fundamental rules of any kind of social life will become a habit. The door will then be wide open for the transition from the first phase of Communist society to its second higher phase, and along with it to the complete withering away of the State.[1]

It is an extraordinary fact that, some two months after writing these lines, Lenin was to find himself occupying the seat of power in St. Petersburg. In as short a time as that the Russian society would be lying at the disposal of the Bolshevik Party over which he presided with a personal authority that was virtually absolute. He would then be like a man who, having lectured for a quarter of a century on the art of bicycle riding, finds himself on a bicycle for the first time in his life.

Less than twenty days after seizing power, the Bolsheviks under Lenin's direction honored the principles he had been advocating by holding free nationwide elections for a Constituent Assembly, which then met in St. Petersburg. At its first session, however, it proved to have an anti-Bolshevik majority, whereupon it was forcibly terminated by armed Bolsheviks, never to meet again. From then on, the Bolsheviks were a minority governing by force. Russia had again become a police state, as it had been under the czars, and would remain one.

Nothing that Lenin had projected worked. In the spring of 1922, sick and disillusioned, he said to the Eleventh Congress of the Russian Communist Party: "The machine tears itself out of our hands: as though there is a man who drives it, but the

[1] Chap. V, Section 4.

machine does not go in the direction it is driven . . . the machine moves not at all as—least of all as—the one who sits at the wheel imagines."[1]

The failure of the Bolshevik régime, which had meant to put into practice the theories of canonical Marxism, produced, like a receivership after bankruptcy, the one-man dictatorship of Josif Stalin.

20

I HAVE PRESENTED Marx's Marxism as a dramatic vision, not as truth. His account of history past had some original insights, but his account of history to come was to be betrayed by the course of history as it actually unfolded after 1848.

The general belief has been, at least until recent times, that the Russian Revolution of November 7, 1917, was a realization of what he had predicted. But it was not that at all. In the first months of 1917 Russia, still under the rule of the feudal aristocracy, was an agricultural society in which the industrial workers, to whom the name "proletariat" has been confined, so far from being "the immense majority" of the population, were a small minority. The revolution of November 7 was nothing like "the proletarian movement . . . , the self-conscious, independent movement of the immense majority," whereby an official bourgeois society, having outlived its time, was to be "sprung into the air." It was, rather, a *coup d'état* by a few conspirators that quickly resolved itself into the arbitrary dictatorship of their clique or faction.

The Chinese Revolution of 1949 bore as little resemblance to the revolution predicted by Marx. So far from being a proletarian revolution at all, it was a peasant uprising, and in the

[1] Fischer, p. 585.

Manifesto Marx had lumped peasants with small manufacturers, shopkeepers, and artisans as "fractions of the middle class." "They are therefore not," he had added, "revolutionary, but conservative. Nay, more; they are reactionary, for they try to roll back the wheel of history."[1] In China since 1949, as in Russia, there has been dictatorial rule by force that does not at all resemble the "dictatorship of the proletariat" described by Marx and Lenin.

What I have just said about Mao Tse-tung's China applies as well to Tito's Yugoslavia, Hoxha's Albania, and Castro's Cuba. In the other countries in which the revolution Marx foresaw is supposed to have taken place, no one even pretends that the proletariat rose up to spring the official society into the air. The so-called dictatorship of the proletariat was imposed on them by the might of Russian arms, and has been maintained by the same agency ever since.

I am not here passing judgment on the régimes that have come to power in Russia, China, Cuba, and the other countries. Here my only point is that these régimes cannot properly be cited as confirming Marx's prediction. Marx's terms, "proletarian revolution" and "dictatorship of the proletariat," have been applied to circumstances different from those he had predicted. If I say there will be an earthquake tomorrow and, instead, there is a thunderstorm, my prediction is not confirmed by calling the thunderstorm an earthquake.

Like Rousseau's *Social Contract*, the writings of Marx, often produced under pressure of time and before the thought had been fully worked out, have their inconsistencies. Perhaps it is a

---

[1] To be sure that I do not mislead by quoting out of context, I give here the sentence that follows the one quoted above: "If by chance they are revolutionary, they are so only in view of their impending transfer into the proletariat; they thus defend not their present, but their future interests; they desert their own standpoint to place themselves at that of the proletariat." In the years leading up to 1949, however, the Chinese peasants who followed Mao Tse-tung were not deserting their own standpoint in view of an "impending transfer into the proletariat."

mistaken impression that, having thought the matter through, he actually expected the second and final revolution of mankind to break out in the France of 1848; for France was then an agricultural country in which those whom he identified as proletarians were in a minority. There is no doubt, however, that he thought the revolution not many years away. In 1850, referring to "how undeveloped the German proletariat still is," he said that "fifteen or twenty or fifty" years might have to elapse before conditions were brought to the point of readiness for the revolution.[1] Writing to Engels in 1857, he said: "I am working like mad all through the nights at putting my economic studies [to be known as his *Grundrisse*] together so that I may at least have the outlines clear before the deluge comes."[2]

Now, in the second half of the twentieth century, it is too late to expect the revolution Marx predicted. The lot of working-men, instead of getting steadily worse with the development of industrialization, as he had said it would, has got steadily better, a process that had begun even before 1848. In the advanced industrial countries, therefore, workingmen have become less revolutionary rather than more, to the point where in the United States their associations are among the conservative elements in the nation. Class warfare has tended to die away rather than become intensified. Moreover, so far from being without national feeling or identity, as Marx said they were, workingmen have showed themselves more nationalistic than class-conscious, so that they have not developed the international class solidarity he predicted.

The typical revolutionaries of our own day, almost a century and a quarter after the *Manifesto*, are not workingmen at all but intellectuals—university teachers, students, writers, and artists —who stand in a posture of alienation and defiance with

[1] In a debate with his opponents in the Communist League. Quoted by Wolfe, p. 484.
[2] Letter of December 8, 1857, in Marx and Engels, *Correspondence, 1846–1895*, p. 225.

respect to what, using the language of 1848, they call "bourgeois society." Their aim is to overthrow that society, and for the most part they assume, in spite of so much experience since the nineteenth century, that what automatically follows will justify the overthrow.

21

IT WAS A CONSTANT embarrassment to Lenin after November 7, 1917, that the proletariat was not a majority in Russia.[1] It may be that, consciously or unconsciously, even Marx and Engels were embarrassed in the latter part of their lives by the failure of the proletariat to become "the immense majority" in the countries where they expected the proletarian revolution to occur soon. I speculate that this accounts for a progressive tendency to substitute the word "people" for "proletariat."

The conception of "the people" is generally thought of in liberal democracies as embracing the entire population. In the context of any revolutionary movement, however, the use of the term has tended to exclude those against whom the movement is directed. The French Revolution was regarded as an uprising of "the people" against the aristocrats, a formulation that made "the people" less than the entire population. Similarly, since the revolutionary movement has been directed against those called bourgeois, the concept of the people has tended to exclude them.

The Marx of the *Manifesto*, moved by the dramatic vision of a society divided into "two great classes directly facing each

---

[1] He was candid about this. In a pamphlet of 1921, *The Crisis in the Party*, he wrote: "A workers government is an abstraction. We in fact have a workers government with, first, this peculiarity, that the peasants, not the workers, constitute a majority of the national population. . . ." Quoted by Fischer, p. 444, from Lenin, *Sochineniya*, 3d ed., XXVI, 87–94.

other," naturally refrained from using the term "people," with the universalistic connotations that clung to it. (We have already seen, in Chapter 16, how he expressed his contempt for the German socialists who thought of themselves as representing "not the interests of the proletariat, but the interests of Human Nature, of Man in general, who belongs to no class, has no reality, who exists only in the realm of philosophical phantasy.") However, in a letter of April 12, 1871, to Dr. Kugelmann he wrote that, before "the next attempt of the French Revolution," after the failure of the attempted revolution in Paris that year, it will be necessary to "shatter" the bureaucratic and military machine as "the preliminary condition of any real people's revolution on the Continent."[1] Perhaps he had in mind, consciously or subconsciously, that neither in France nor on the Continent as a whole was the proletariat in a majority. By using the more comprehensive term "people," he avoided the question this raised.

Lenin, in *The State and Revolution,* seized on this. "This idea of a 'people's' revolution," he wrote, "seems strange on Marx's lips. And the Russian Plekhanovists and Mensheviks . . . might possibly consider such an expression a slip of the tongue. . . . On the continent of Europe, in 1871, the proletariat did not in a single country constitute the majority of the people. A 'people's' revolution, actually sweeping the majority into its current, could be such only if embracing both the proletariat and the peasantry. Both classes then constituted the 'people.'. . . Consequently, when speaking of 'a real people's revolution,' Marx did not in the least forget the peculiar characteristics of the lower middle classes [the category in which he had placed the peasants.]"[2] A few pages after having given this explanation, Lenin was thereby enabled to refer to the Paris Commune as a "proletarian democracy" that represented "the suppression of

---

[1] Marx, 1934, p. 309.
[2] Chap. III, Section 1.

the oppressors by the whole force of the majority of the nation—the proletariat and the peasants."[1] Again, after referring to the peasantry [and] other sections of the lower middle class," he wrote: "The great majority of peasants in all capitalist countries where the peasant class does exist . . . are oppressed by the Government and long for its overthrow. . . . This hope can only be realized by the proletariat. . . ."[2] In other words, the proletariat will make the revolution and set up its dictatorship on behalf of proletariat and peasantry alike, the two groups together constituting a majority called "the people."

It is understandable that, since Lenin's day, the vaguer term "people" has largely replaced "the proletariat" in the language of the communist followers of Marx and Lenin. Lenin referred to his Bolshevik government as "the dictatorship of the proletariat," but a generation later it would have been hard to find any Communist in official position who used the term in reference to the régimes in Moscow, Peking, Sofia, Bucharest, Tirana, Belgrade, Budapest, Prague, Warsaw, Pankow, Hanoi, or Havana. All except two of these régimes presided over what were called "people's republics," Moscow and Havana being the exceptions, for the reasons that the first had come into being before the term came into fashion, while the second had decided only after it had already been in being some years that it was a Marxist-Leninist régime.

At the same time, linguistic usage in the communist world has tended to substitute for Marx's two great and opposed classes, the bourgeoisie and the proletariat, another set of opponents: "the people" and "the enemies of the people."

I commented earlier (Chapter 16, first footnote) that the terms "bourgeoisie" and "proletariat" were not definable as the term "man" is. "People" and "enemies of the people," however, are terms that, when coupled, lend themselves to such a wide

---

[1] Chap. IV, Section 2.
[2] Chap. III, Section 2.

range of usage, all of it artificial, as to make the terms they have replaced seem, by comparison, models of scientific precision. An objective census taker, allowing himself some arbitrary license (which would not be necessary if he were counting only "man"), could count the respective numbers of "the bourgeoisie" and "the proletariat" in a particular society. He would, however, have to receive very special instructions indeed, *ad hoc* instructions for each case, if he were to count the respective numbers of "the people" and "the enemies of the people." There is reason to believe that, alike in Hungary in November 1956, and in Czechoslovakia in August 1968, "the enemies of the people," from Moscow's point of view, constituted the immense majority.

When Marx and later Lenin referred to "the bourgeoisie" and "the proletariat" they were referring to social classes generally identifiable by their occupations, by their respective relationships to the modes of economic production. But "people" and "enemies of the people" are not social classes at all. How can one identify them in a "people's republic" unless by whether they bow to the governing régime or oppose it?

If, in fact, the proletariat is the ruling class in these countries, there is less said about it as time passes. To call the régimes in Peking, Hanoi, Tirana, Havana, and the other capitals "dictatorships of the proletariat" would be to raise questions that, from their point of view, had better not be raised.

One of these questions would be about the withering away of the state.

22

MARX HAD WRITTEN in the *Manifesto* that "when, in the course of development, class distinctions have disappeared, and

all production has been concentrated in the hands of a vast association of the whole nation, the public power will lose its political character."

In his *Anti-Dühring*, originally published in London in 1878, Engels wrote:

> The first act by virtue of which the State really constitutes itself the representative of the whole society—the taking possession of the means of production in the name of society—this is, at the same time, its last independent act as a State. State interference in social relations becomes, in one domain after another, superfluous, and then withers away of itself; the government of persons is replaced by the administration of things, and by the conduct of processes of production. The State is not "abolished." *It withers away.*[1]

In *The State and Revolution* Lenin wrote that "the proletariat, according to Marx, needs only a withering away State—a State, that is, so constituted that it begins to wither away immediately, and cannot but wither away. . . ."[2] Again, he writes that the *Manifesto* "brings us to the necessary conclusion . . . that this proletarian State must begin to wither away immediately after its victory. . . ."[3]

Lenin, interpreting Marx, does not say that the state will "immediately" disappear upon the seizure of power by the proletariat. He does say that it will "immediately" begin to wither away.

In the same work, Lenin also addresses himself to the question of how long it will take the state to wither away. "It is clear," he writes, "that there can be no question of defining the exact moment of the *future* 'withering away'—the more so as it must obviously be a prolonged process."[4] Again: "we are right in speaking solely of the inevitable withering away of the State, emphasizing the protracted nature of the process, and its

[1] Engels, 1959, p. 387.
[2] Chap. II, Section 1.
[3] Chap. II, Section 1.
[4] Chap. V, Section 1.

dependence upon the rapidity of development of the *higher phase* of Communism; leaving quite open the question of lengths of time, or the concrete forms of this withering away, since material for the solution of such questions is not available."[1]

There is no ambiguity here: (1) the withering away will begin "immediately," and (2) it will be prolonged. Lenin said this just before he himself assumed the responsibility for the "proletarian" seizure of power and the setting up of "the dictatorship of the proletariat." Four months later, challenged at the Seventh Party Congress to say something about the coming statelessness, he answered that "to proclaim in advance the withering away of the State would be to destroy the perspective of history."[2] On July 11, 1919, in a lecture to the students of Moscow's Sverdlov University, he said: "We have taken this apparatus [i.e., the state] away from the capitalists, taken it for ourselves. With this apparatus or with a club we shall smash all exploitation, and when no possibility of exploitation remains on the earth, when there are no more owners of land, owners of factories, when it will no longer be true that some eat their fill while others starve —only then, when no such possibility remains, will we scrap this apparatus."[3] Here Lenin was saying that the state would not, after all, wither away of itself. In a remote eschatological future, when the kingdom of heaven had been attained on earth, then "will we scrap this apparatus."

Neither in Soviet Russia nor in the other societies that are supposedly carrying out the program projected by Marx has the prospect that the state will wither away become more imminent since Lenin's day. What is nominally the purgatorial and purgative period of transition foreseen by Marx has become, one suspects, permanent.

Nowhere has Marx's program been realized in any of its

---

[1] Chap. V, Section 4.
[2] Fischer, p. 257.
[3] Fischer, pp. 369–370.

essential aspects. Nowhere has the proletariat, after becoming the immense majority of the population, overthrown the rule of the bourgeoisie and established its dictatorship. Nowhere have the workers taken over the administration of society. Nowhere has the state begun to wither away. Instead of this, cliques of political adventurers or charismatic leaders, whether with good intentions or bad, have established slave states that, while often ministering to the welfare of elements in their populations that were formerly downtrodden, have stifled freedom. I do not here raise the question whether this is a good thing or not. I merely point out that it is not what Marx predicted and called for.

23

M ARX HAD A VISION of the future that the future failed to bear out. If we are to learn the lesson of this failure we must resist the temptation to say that the failure was not in the prophecy but in the way things went in the real world, that the future was wrong. We must resist the temptation to say that, if governments had not happened to introduce reforms when they did, or if Lenin had not chosen the wrong moment to make the revolution in Russia, or if Stalin had not upset everything, we would have seen how right Marx's prophecy was.

The basic fault, surely, was in Marx's conception. Specifically, it was in his belief that men, rather than constituting one species with a common human nature, are divided into two species quite different from each other. His original view of mankind as one "species being," the individual members of which are torn by inner conflict, represented true understanding, the understanding that has been the basis of our greatest humanitarian literature from the ancient Greeks through Shakespeare to

Dostoyevsky and Tolstoy. In the end, however, his Manichean disposition overbore his philosophical insight. His departure from the reality of one human nature is summed up in the single sentence of the *Manifesto* in which he attacked the German socialists for taking pride in the thought that they were "representing, . . . not the interests of the proletariat, but the interests of Human Nature, of Man in general, who belongs to no class, has no reality, who exists only in the misty realm of philosophical phantasy." The basis of the difference between the philosophical Marxism in the manuscripts of 1844 and the Marxism of the *Manifesto* is in the conception of social classes as constituting distinct species. In the society that he saw as divided between "two great classes directly facing each other" there was no such thing as "human nature." Instead, there was bourgeois nature on the one hand, proletarian nature on the other.

The Manichean disposition of Marx's nature—and, if I may put it that way, of our common human nature—led him and his followers to distinguish his two classes as the demons and the angels. The popular appeal that this gave to the Marxism of the *Manifesto* was paid for by the sacrifice of truth.

One may plausibly believe that more than Marx's Manicheism entered into the creation of the myth of the wicked bourgeois and the good proletarian. He had ended his *Theses on Feuerbach* in 1845 with the statement, "The philosophers have only *interpreted* the world in different ways, the point is to *change* it." The change he had in mind was to take the form of another French Revolution in which the downtrodden masses would rise up and, in one convulsive movement, overthrow their rulers. The struggle of the good people against the wicked might be expected to move the masses as a more realistic and sophisticated interpretation of the world never could. Marx had, in effect, avowed his willingness to sacrifice fidelity of interpretation to the objective of change. This meant, in a word, the

sacrifice of truth. No one, however, makes this sacrifice without himself being the victim. Even though one does not say what one believes, one believes what one says. I see no reason to doubt that Marx, Engels, and Lenin, once their minds had been finally formed, assumed without questioning that there was a wicked species called the bourgeoisie and a good one called the proletariat.

The application of the fallacy of the two species to partisan politics is virtually universal. Evil is inherent in politics no matter who practices it. The necessity of government, itself, as Hobbes understood, is the consequence of those socially dangerous elements in every one of us that we identify as evil. Government is the exercise of power over society, and the art of exercising such power is the art of politics. It is a competitive art practiced by ambitious men who, for reasons good or bad, aspire to power. Every society tries to limit, by constitutional or customary inhibitions, the means that the contestants use in their mutual competition, thereby making the struggle less savage than it would otherwise be. In the most advanced and self-disciplined societies, for example, such Byzantine devices as the kidnapping, torturing, or killing of one's political opponents are ruled out. Even at its best, however, the practice of politics involves conspiracy, betrayal of one's word, double-dealing, and a certain ruthlessness when it comes to personal relations.

All this is inescapable in the present state of the world. Despite popular legend to the contrary, even Abraham Lincoln and Mahatma Gandhi repeatedly violated the moral principles for which they stood in the pursuit of their political careers. (Lincoln, for example, to gain the acceptance of the Emancipation Proclamation, had to enter into some unquestionably sordid deals with politicians from the Southern border states.) The plain fact is that men in politics are constantly faced with a choice among evils only, so that whatever choice they make is evil. It is true that a man in a position of political responsibility

can avoid the choice by resigning, thereby leaving others to make it, but the choice would still have to be made and the evil accepted.

According to Christian tradition, the chief manifestation of the original sin by which we are all marked is our sexual appetite. I, myself, would sooner say it was the practice of politics, which is equally indispensable to our survival.

All of us are aware of the evil with which the practice of government is permeated. If asked to account for it, however, most of us would reply by explaining that politicians were unprincipled by nature, or that those who occupied the seats of power were a pack of scoundrels. Implicit in this reply would be the thesis that, if we or people like us were in power, matters would be different. This is one form that the fallacy of the two species takes. As in all its forms, it opposes the abstraction of a high-principled and idealistic "we" to the abstraction of an unscrupulous and self-serving "they."

The irresistible and unresisted fallacy of the two species accounts, I think, for the practical failure of Lenin, which was also the failure of Marx and Engels. In their Manichean vision, bourgeois government was evil because it was government by the wicked. Proletarian government, being government by the virtuous, would naturally be quite different: it would be directed by persons ("the armed workers," according to Lenin) with a common and selfless dedication to the service of society, who would strive together, shoulder to shoulder, to advance the day when they could give up their exercise of power as no longer necessary.

Surely this explains Lenin's curiously naive belief, as late as the summer of 1917, that when the proletariat took power politics would disappear from the conduct of government. In "most of the more progressive capitalist countries," as he put it:

> it is quite possible, immediately, within twenty-four hours, to pass to the overthrow of the capitalists and bureaucrats, and to

replace them, in the control of production and distribution, in the business of apportioning labor and products, by the armed workers, or the people in arms. The question of control and book-keeping must not be confused with the question of the scientifically educated staff of engineers, agriculturalists, and so on. These gentlemen work today owing allegiance to the capitalists: they will work even better tomorrow, owing it to the armed workers. Book-keeping and control—these are the chief things necessary for the smooth and correct functioning of the *first phase* of communist society. *All* the citizens are here transformed into the hired employees of the State, which then is the armed workers. . . . The book-keeping and control necessary for this have been simplified by capitalism to the utmost, till they have become the extraordinarily simple operations of watching, recording, and issuing receipts, within the reach of anybody who can read and write and knows the first four arithmetical rules.[1]

Lenin appears never to have doubted that any petty considerations of self-interest would be unknown to "the armed workers," who would show themselves perfect in wisdom and judgment. For twenty-four years he had been engaged in the fierce political combat of the Russian Marxists for control of the movement, a combat in which he had proved himself the ablest of all, as well as the most ruthless, yet he still allowed himself to believe that the factional politics of which he had such intimate experience would not continue after the movement gained control of the Russian state.

The paradoxical co-existence in one person of worldly wisdom and naiveté is common to all sophisticated men who live by a simple faith, whether religious or ideological. Such men appear to be able to exclude the application of their critical faculties, however active and well developed, from the area of their faith.

What prevented the fulfillment of Lenin's Marxist faith, after the *coup* of November 1917, was our common human nature, that nature of "man in general" to which Marx had denied the status of reality.

[1] Lenin, 1919, Chap. V, Section 4.

The fulfillment in Russia of the faith with which he had so wholly identified himself meant that he had, by whatever devices, to maintain his own personal power at the helm of the Russian state. The maintenance of his personal power required, in turn, that the Bolshevik party, although it proved to be in a minority, retain its rule over the Russian empire; therefore he had it use armed force to disperse the anti-Bolshevik Constituent Assembly. At every turning, after that, the requirements that the retention of power itself imposed overrode the ideological principles, which proved inapplicable.[1] When, exhausted by the political struggle, he began to lose his own power, others in the party leadership conspired against him and one another to achieve more power for themselves or simply to hold on to what they had. In this contest, not the man who was the most dedicated to the Marxist program, but the man who was the most adept and unscrupulous in playing the politics of power, came out on top and established his personal dictatorship.

24

IN THE FIRST chapter I said I was concerned with ideology only in the narrow sense of the term, as signifying systems of

[1] They proved inapplicable in more than this alone. In the summer of 1921, twenty-five million people in the Volga Valley alone were starving. Karl Radek, a member of Lenin's government, asked if there was any danger of the party's degenerating or being transformed, replied: "Certainly, we are being transformed daily. In Switzerland, as revolutionary exiles, we never paid any attention to rainfall, being preoccupied by Marxian discussions. And now we are more concerned with rainfall and drought than with the philosophy of Mach and Avenarius. Osinsky, the present Commissar of Agriculture, was then translating Verlaine, and was totally indifferent to ploughing and sowing. Now he is obsessed by agriculture, and fights only with locusts and other pests. Kissilov used to be absorbed in plans for annoying the bourgeoisie; now all his thoughts are given to the proper organization of the Moscow tramways. . . . In former days we thought a bourgeois only worth wiping out; now we wonder if he will make a good factory director." Quoted by Fischer, p. 508, from Farbman, p. 303.

belief that were implicitly totalitarian. I then drew a contrast between two opposed conceptions of how society should be organized: the liberal, based on the accommodation of diversity, and the totalitarian, based on the imposition of conformity.

There is a paradox in the association of communism with the latter, because the Marxist scriptures on which it is officially based envisaged a society "in which," as the *Manifesto* had it, "the free development of each is the condition for the free development of all." This promised land, however, was said to lie beyond a Slough of Despond called "the dictatorship of the proletariat," and the danger was, surely, that struggling human- ity, once in the Slough, would never emerge from it. In those states that call themselves communist, "the dictatorship of the proletariat" has, in fact, become the permanent dictatorship of a party, a clique, or an individual, ruling in the name of "the people" and persecuting, as "enemies of the people," any who do not conform to the views and conduct that it labels "correct."

It is clear that the broad class of professional revolutionaries to which Marx, Engels, and Lenin belonged was preoccupied with the negative aim of destroying the established organization of society, of overthrowing the privileged class or classes of that society, and of destroying the state that upheld the existing conditions. The anarchists were explicit in denying any need to be concerned with what might follow such destruction. The Marxists concerned themselves with it only secondarily, pre- senting a myth of purgatory and salvation to justify them in the destruction that was their immediate objective.

This is normal. The negative comes more easily to most of us than the positive. The animus behind any revolutionary move- ment is opposition to things as they are. Revolutionaries are driven by an indignation that may be well founded, or are driven by frustration and hatred, to destroy what seems to them abominable. They would hardly be human if they addressed themselves with equal seriousness and zeal to the less immediate

task of concocting in the imagination some alternative that would be workable, even though, in concocting it, they had to disregard as unworthy all previous human experience. No wonder they evaded the problem by postulating a transformation of human nature that would make it go away.

Lenin, in 1917, was troubled by the necessity of justifying to himself and others the fact that he was proceeding to make "the proletarian revolution" in a country where the preconditions considered necessary for its success had not yet developed. The basis on which he went ahead anyway is revealed by his citation of Napoleon's maxim: "One engages oneself, and then one sees."[1] Castro's animus was against the sordid Cuban dictatorship of Batista, and when he addressed himself to the question of what he would put in its place, if he succeeded in overthrowing it, he described a Jeffersonian régime with free elections and a capitalist economy. After he did succeed, however, circumstances he had not anticipated dictated what he actually would put in its place.[2]

The professional revolutionaries pursue their aim of destroying the existing order by fomenting disorder. In the constant and ubiquitous tension between order and chaos they engage themselves on the side of chaos. As between order and chaos, however, chaos cannot ultimately win because, as Hobbes knew, it is intolerable. When people find themselves deprived of the protection of a social organization that is able to keep order, when they find themselves at the mercy of criminals and street mobs, their persons, their families, and their homes exposed to every outrage that superior force can commit, they will embrace any alternative. They will prefer slavery to such freedom. Therefore, when a society that is breaking down in disorder

[1] Cited by Wolfe, p. 296. While it is possible to make too much of the fact that Napoleon, following this maxim, engaged himself on the road to Waterloo, it is not irrelevant.

[2] See Halle, 1967, pp. 401–403. These pages are relevant not only to the example of Dr. Castro but to the theme of this chapter.

approaches the condition of chaos, its members turn for salvation to such rule as seemed to Hobbes without alternative.

The increasing disorder that represented the breakdown of the Roman republic was resolved by the dictatorship of Augustus Caesar. The increasing disorder that represented the breakdown of the French monarchy was resolved by the dictatorship of Bonaparte. The increasing disorder consequent upon the breakdown of the czarist régime was resolved by the dictatorship that Lenin had never intended. The increasing disorder of Germany under the Weimar Republic was resolved by Hitler's dictatorship.

Those who work for chaos in the belief that it leads to freedom are likely to find, if successful, that they were mistaken.

25

THE DOCTRINAIRE revolutionary movements that we call "left-wing" nominally uphold the ideal of anarchy (except where they have come into power). They uphold the ideal of the stateless society in which individual freedom is maximized. By contrast, the movements called "right-wing" tend, in their degree, to glorify the state and to stand for the disciplined regimentation of those who are under its jurisdiction. At their totalitarian extreme, to which the label "fascist" applies, the individual is expected, ideally, to abnegate his individuality altogether, living only for the service of the state.

The ideal of the individual who submits himself, body and mind, to the direction of the state responds to the revulsion of so many individuals against the loneliness and responsibility implicit in individual freedom. The loneliness is passionately expressed by Rousseau in the opening lines of his *Confessions*

(from which I quoted in Chapter 10). He feels himself different from any other being that ever was or will be. Therefore he stands alone, confronting an alien world, and has to bear by himself the perplexing responsibility of making his own decisions. For many individuals, the loneliness and responsibility constitute too high a price to pay for personal freedom. (This, surely, is what explains the appeal, for the solitary man who wrote the *Social Contract*, of the imagined state that relieves the individual of his individuality, reducing him to a mere cell in the body politic.)

The free individual feels himself, moreover, too small to cope with the immensity of the world in which he finds himself. Alone, he is no more than a mite in a maelstrom. Because his individual identity seems so insufficient, he feels the need to adopt, by association, another identity that represents the greatness and power he lacks. In ancient times, a man who was nothing by himself became great, in his own esteem and that of others, by being able to say: "*Civis Romanus sum.*"

Every society must, it seems to me, provide for those individuals who are not prepared to bear the burden of freedom. In fact, every society does. Anyone who has served in the lowest military ranks knows how many soldiers have adopted the profession to escape the burden. In an army the individual is fed, clothed, and sheltered (the army is his shepherd, he shall not want), and, by making the decisions for him, it spares him from having to determine the conduct of his life for himself. Many privates feel themselves happiest where they are, and would resist promotion.

The function of providing for those who do not want to be free has also been performed by monasteries and convents in times past. It is partially performed by fraternal orders, such as the Masons, and it is understandable that such orders have been particularly prevalent in the United States, where individual freedom has traditionally been greater than elsewhere.

The function is also performed by communist parties and other conspiratorial organizations that put their members under discipline. Finally, it is performed in a lesser degree by those political movements that, although not imposing discipline, have the allegiance that their members give them out of the need to think what others think rather than think their own thoughts in the loneliness of their own minds.

The accelerating expansion and complication of modern societies, in consequence of technological developments, has in itself been increasing the loneliness of the individual, the perplexity of his responsibilities, and the sense of his inadequacy. If it is to be expected that, in addition to managing his individual affairs within the individual sphere that is his, as a citizen he will also take responsible positions on the great matters of foreign and domestic policy which present themselves for national decision, then he cannot fulfill the expectation. Because freedom is not to be separated from responsibility, he has more freedom than he can exercise. He ends by giving it away.

Earlier I made the point, to which I shall return, that the surges of right-wing radicalism occur in response to the threat of social disorder posed by the radicalism of the left. As we have just seen, however, the radicalism of the right has independent roots in a revulsion of mortal men against the increasing burden of freedom. Moreover, while it does not have such a broad philosophical background as left-wing radicalism, it does indirectly have some background in the thought of those philosophers who, since Plato, have exalted the state.

26

IF WE AGREE that anarchism pursues an unrealizable dream, it makes no sense to think in terms of being for or against the

state as such. A state of some kind is necessary to define and police the rules that must govern relations among the members of any society. The only question that arises is: what kind of state?

Those who have most mistrusted human nature when left to itself have therefore favored an authoritarian state, while those who have taken a sanguine view of it have felt the less hesitation in favoring a state that has no other function than to regulate and police freedom. Again, however, the either-or question, whether human nature is good or bad, does not fit reality. Depending on circumstances, human nature varies from one extreme to the other. Education may produce a self-disciplined human nature, or people may exercise self-discipline because they live in a community so small that everyone knows everyone else. People who are reasonable and gentle as individuals acting on their own responsibility, as such, may go wild when, surrendering their individuality by merging themselves in a mass, they escape individual accountability and, with it, the sense of individual responsibility. Different normative ideas produce different manifestations of human nature. Thus many of the Japanese have shown themselves gentle and considerate in one decade while, in another, under the domination of normative ideas promoted by ideological extremists, the same individuals have shown themselves aggressive and cruel. The Germans, too, have demonstrated how people of good will can become savage under the influence of ideology.

Plato, in the *Republic*, favored an authoritarian state because he had himself experienced, in the breakdown of Athenian democracy, the failure of the self-governing people to use their freedom responsibly. Hobbes similarly favored an authoritarian state because he had experienced, in the English civil wars, the immoderation of ideologically motivated multitudes. On the other hand, in modern times Americans, British, Scandinavians, Swiss, and others have, at least until our own day, justified the

sanguine views of Locke and Jefferson by a sufficiently self-disciplined exercise of freedom.

I think we must conclude that the question whether human nature is such that people, living together in society, can be entrusted with freedom does not depend on some invariable human nature that exists independently of a social context. It depends, rather, on the social context itself. There are times when particular peoples are ready for freedom, but its enjoyment and its constant widening may at last lead to a relaxation of the inner discipline that had made it possible, until the point comes when disorder produces breakdown, and freedom is no longer possible.

In the preceding paragraphs, assuming that freedom is good in itself, I touched only on the circumstances that make it possible or impossible. As we have seen, however, it imposes a burden on the individual that many are not prepared to bear, so that they deliberately renounce it by entering military service, by joining religious orders, by putting themselves under the discipline of an ideological movement, or by becoming part of a mass. As life grows more complex and confusing, there are undoubtedly more and more people moved by a nihilism that has for its real objective, even though they do not recognize it themselves, the elimination of a freedom that puts them under too great a strain. This motive for favoring an authoritarian state, different from the one Plato and Hobbes had, is represented by the Rousseau whose longing to have the state relieve him of the burden of his individuality has its poignant expression in the *Social Contract*.

The revolt against freedom, which can be traced back so far, is associated with a revolt against reason that, developing in the nineteenth century, represented a reaction against the preceding "age of reason." In the romantic Rousseau, who anticipated the nineteenth and twentieth centuries in more than one respect, the revolt against reason is at least foreshadowed by his disposition

to give sentiment primacy, to evaluate actions and experiences according to the subjective emotions with which they are associated.

Hegel, whose life was lived half in the eighteenth and half in the nineteenth century, made passion a prime motive force in the dialectic by which God or mankind progressed toward self-realization, and to that extent he endorsed it, but he made reason the foundation of being. He equated God or "the Absolute Idea" with the rational, and he regarded history as the rational realizing itself.

Hegel's younger contemporary, Schopenhauer, deliberately took issue with this, insisting that life was the expression of a blind will rather than of reason.

All idea [he wrote], of whatever kind it may be, all *object*, is *phenomenal* existence, but the *will* alone is a *thing-in-itself*. As such, it is throughout not idea, but *toto genere* different from it; it is that of which all idea, all object, is the phenomenal appearance, the visibility, the objectification. It is the inmost nature, the kernel, of every particular thing, and also of the whole. It appears in every blind force of nature and also in the pre-considered action of man; and the great difference between these two is merely in the degree of the manifestation, not in the nature of what manifests itself.[1]

The belief in will rather than reason as the driving force received a notable impetus from the publication in 1859 of Darwin's *Origin of Species*, which gave rise to the popular conception of a dramatic struggle among species from which only "the fittest" emerged still alive. It was easy to picture international relations as such a struggle among states, rather than species, and to exalt will as a prime factor in determining the outcome. Again, Nietzsche gave primacy to "the will to power," and although he would not have agreed with some of the uses that were made of this conception in the twentieth century, just as he would not have agreed with the debasement of his idea

[1] Schopenhauer, Book II, Section 21.

of the Übermensch, it did deny the primacy that had previously been given to reason. In the twentieth century, D. H. Lawrence would campaign against the primacy of the rational intellect and in favor of "instinct," of "thinking with the blood"; and Sigmund Freud would create a mythology according to which all human beings were governed by dark unconscious drives that represented the antithesis of reason.

Finally, Georges Sorel represented the revolt against reason in terms that bore directly on the political organization of society. He promoted some of the conceptual antecedents of right-wing radicalism, without himself being a right-wing radical. An admirer of Lenin, he lived long enough to rejoice in the approaching triumph of Italian fascism, dying two months before Mussolini's "March on Rome." He was opposed to intellectuality, to the rational uses of the mind, to the serious formulation of responsible programs for the future. He was in favor of myths that deceive and of irrationality. Above all, he was in favor of social violence as the only means of generating an heroic mortality. Having reasoned against reason, he prepared the way for those who would act against it.

27

FASCIST MOVEMENTS, being anti-intellectual, have lacked such a foundation of philosophical reasoning as has made the movements called communist respectable in the eyes of intellectuals. In the case of communism, the philosophy came first. The *Manifesto*, itself, was simply the translation of a philosophy into a program of political action. Fascist movements, by contrast, laid hold of what they could to cover their philosophical nakedness after they were already well grown. They retained the services of philosophers or philosophizers (e.g., Alfredo Rocco,

Giovanni Gentile, Alfred Rosenberg) to design philosophical clothing, just as they retained the services of costume designers to design uniforms for the leaders of the movements and their cohorts.

What the fascist movements lacked in philosophy they made up in theater. It is surely no accident that the extreme of fascism was realized in the two countries most notable for their contributions to grand opera. Mussolini, assuming the part of "Il Duce," had himself outfitted with special costumes. On the balcony of the Palazzo Venezia, before the packed square, he lifted his voice in crescendo to a pitch of passion barely controlled, reaching out his right arm above the audience as if the shaking fist held thunderbolts. At last, when his voice fell, when his two hands came to rest on his hips, the applause of the audience, the stamping of feet, and the cries of "Bravo!" rose into the Roman skies. For the moment, politics had been exalted to the heroic plane on which Georges Sorel had dreamed it might someday be. Anyone witnessing the scene could testify, then, how greatly sentiment ("thinking with the blood") transcended the sterile operations of the reasoning intellect.

It is fitting that the precursor of Mussolini was that poet and lover, to whom the contemporary goddess of the theater, Eleanora Duse, had surrendered herself, Gabriele d'Annunzio, Prince of Monte Nevoso. D'Annunzio, with his chorus of volunteers, had captured Fiume in what proved to be a rehearsal for Mussolini's "March on Rome." A disciple of Nietzsche, d'Annunzio was also an admirer of Richard Wagner —and Wagner, the man of the theater, more than any philosopher, was a source of inspiration for Adolf Hitler.

It follows that to understand the Nazi movement, in turn, one should go to *Der Ring der Nibelungen* in preference to the writings of any philosopher. German opera is greater in scale and weight than Italian, requiring a bigger stage. On the stage that the Nazis provided, the ocean of storm troopers extended to

the horizon, while the tall, blood-red pennons with their swastikas, rank upon rank, stood above it like the multitudinous sails of Viking fleets awaiting the order to move forward. Never had choruses so large been assembled on a stage so extensive. When they shouted their pagan cries in unison it was like the earth, itself, speaking. And then, just when the suspense threatened to become too great, the leader who had been invoked by the ritualistic repetition of his name from so many throats appeared at the center of the scene, the focal point of myriad arms raised like bayonets in salute. Out of the hush that followed spoke the voice of the Führer, proclaiming the world-historical mission of a new master race.

To the decadence of an overripe civilization in the Atlantic world, with its physical softness and moral lethargy, fascism in Italy opposed the warlike virtue of the early Romans who had made the Mediterranean their own sea, not hesitating to spit Carthaginian babies on their swords in the service of so great a purpose. To the decadence of that same civilization, National Socialism in Germany opposed the warlike virtue of the old Teutonic tribes who had triumphed over the Romans when at last it had been their turn to lose their virile qualities. The ideal of the warrior-hero who glories in violence was restored. Italian clerks were told that they were world conquerors. Little German shopkeepers were stirred by the revelation that the blood of Siegfried coursed in their veins.

In the actual conduct of Fascists and Nazis alike, the detached observer might have found it difficult to distinguish what presented itself as the heroism of old from the behavior of modern gangsters. World War I had left Italy in disorder, its people convinced that the fruits of victory had been taken out of their hands, its workers unemployed, its peasants hungry, many of its demobilized soldiers ranging in quest of adventure, left-wing radicals threatening revolution, and a government unable to govern. In these circumstances, Mussolini's black-shirted

ruffians spread terror in city and countryside, using the tactics of the Mafia to intimidate the opposition and the representatives of legality. Mussolini openly avowed that he had no program, that his objective was simply to get the government for himself. Those in Rome who had to make the decision whether to surrender it finally came to the conclusion that the best way to secure the country from the threat he posed was to adopt the principle of appointing the wolf protector of the lamb. The King of Italy, with due formality, handed the country over to him.

By continuing assassination and intimidation, then, combined with the outward forms of grand opera, Mussolini proceeded to transform Italy into a totalitarian state. Having done this, he undertook to transform the Italian people, themselves, into a nation of warriors who would march forth for the establishment of a new Roman empire over the sea that he now called *"mare nostrum."*

If the end of the Fascist reign, after some twenty-three years, was sordid and ludicrous, it was also unforeseen. Mussolini's achievement was that for most of those years he succeeded in making semblance serve for reality. In Italy, and not only in Italy, people believed. This is one of the properties of ideology. In Russia, too, the semblance of proletarian revolution and proletarian rule had been made to serve for the reality. In Russia, too, and not only in Russia, people had believed.

It would have been hard to find any leavening of the ludicrous in the parallel history of the National Socialist movement in Germany, so much greater was its scale, its scope, and its destruction. It, too, was born of humiliation and disorder following World War I, and came to power when it seemed that the government of the Weimar Republic, unable to cope adequately with the economic crisis of the nineteen-thirties, might also be unable to hold back the rising sea of disorder and left-wing radicalism. Hitler's National Socialism, too, used gangster tactics of terrorism and intimidation to have the government and people of Ger-

many entrusted to his keeping. He, too, then constructed a totalitarian state organized for war, and set out to establish the Teutonic dominion on earth that he had written into the libretto entitled *Mein Kampf.*

Hitler's state lasted twelve terrible years, and as its enemies finally closed in on it he ordered the last and greatest of all his operatic gestures. While the state which he had said was built to last a thousand years went under, like another *Titanic* sinking beneath the Atlantic waves, its radio stations broadcast the music of Wagner's *Götterdämmerung,* "The Twilight of the Gods."

One may well ask, at this point, why the fascist régimes were never able to establish themselves on a lasting basis, by contrast with the régimes that call themselves communist.

28

Mussolini's fascist régime in Italy and Hitler's National Socialist régime in Germany did not endure, as the communist régimes have endured, because they were overthrown in war. It is hard to believe, however, that this end to their careers was accidental, that it might not have occurred. The primary cause of their downfall, surely, was a sowing of the wind to which the reaping of the whirlwind was secondary. The two régimes—having dethroned reason to enthrone, in its place, the will to power—had no choice but to drive the nations under their sway toward the conflagration of war. Bonaparte's career, someone remarked, was like that of a bicycle rider: if he stops he falls. The basis on which Mussolini and Hitler came to power was in their promises to make their respective countries great through war. Each could hold his power only by a convulsive mobiliza-

tion of the entire population and all the material resources of the
nation for the realization of an objective so grand as to intoxicate
the people with a vision of national destiny. Having mobilized
them, he could not stop there.

In a besieged city the population may accept regimentation
and hardship because it seems the only alternative to the extinction of the society, perhaps to physical extinction as well. The
Russian dictatorship, in the years after the Revolution, was able
to persuade the Russian people that such was their case. Mao
Tse-tung's dictatorship in China and Castro's in Cuba were each
able to persuade their respective peoples that they were in a
state of siege, their independence at stake. But no case could be
made, in the interwar period, that Italy or Germany was besieged
and had to adopt desperate measures for its survival. The only
alternative, then, was to intoxicate the people with dreams of
grandeur and glory. This was the more easily done where the
people, especially the young, were in a state of inner rebellion
against the slimness and sordidness of what life appeared to hold
for them otherwise.

Promising the people enlargement from their confines, promising them emergence into a sunnier sphere where they could
enact the ancient heroism they felt within them, promising them
that they should be as the Romans had been a thousand years
earlier, as the British had been in the nineteenth century,
Mussolini and Hitler drove on to their own inevitable destruction. It is not under all circumstances that, having mobilized a
country for war, one can then refrain from going to war. If
either dictator stopped he would fall.

At first, before enough external resistance built up against
him, each had his successes: Mussolini in the Dodecanese
Islands, in Corfu, in Albania, and in Ethiopia; Hitler in the Saar,
in the Rhineland, in Austria, and in Czechoslovakia. However,
because the dynamics of their expansion was such that (as in the
case of Bonaparte) there was no point at which either could stop

of his own decision, and because such a course of expansion was by its nature unlimited, all the threatened nations of the world were bound to combine against them, at last, in a common defence.

Mussolini posed the emptier threat, lacking by so much as he did a geographical and demographic base that would support his pretentions. Surely, however, Hitler's Third Reich was equally doomed. Even if it had overcome Russia and Britain it would not have been able to stabilize its position and make peace. It would not have been able to pacify the peoples under its rule, from Vladivostok to the Atlantic, and across the Atlantic it would have found itself confronting the aroused might of North America. The consequence of its victory would have been a fatal overextension of its power; it would have found itself entangled in a continuing warfare to which no end could be foreseen short of its own exhaustion and defeat. (This conclusion is not affected by the fact that, in such circumstances, it might have dragged the whole world of civilization down to ruin with it.) Hitler's Reich could at any time lose the war, but could never finally win it.

The very conception of a nation organized for permanent war had become obsolete in the twentieth century because of the exhausting and destructive character that modern war had assumed. The day was over when savage tribes, living under the most primitive economic circumstances, could engage in perpetual warfare with their neighbors. The day was gone when nations could entrust the making of war to small professional armies while they went about their normal peacetime business. Now, when all the resources of a nation were mobilized for war, war could only be a spasm of limited duration, ending in exhaustion and destruction beyond repair if it went on too long.

Today, with nuclear weapons poised, in effect, over every country on earth, it is not conceivable that a Mussolini or

Hitler could again win any important part of a great nation to the acceptance of a policy of expansion by military conquest.

The question that has been raised is why the fascist régimes, unlike the communist, were never able to establish themselves on a lasting basis. We can see now, what was not apparent in the nineteen-thirties, that their dependence on war was self-defeating. But their dependence on war was itself a consequence of the fact that the fascist ideology lacked an adequate foundation, that it was without roots in history, literature, or philosophy.

The foundations of every ideology are false, in the sense that every ideology bases itself on some vision of the world that does not correspond to existential reality. The original Marxism, as we have seen, was as completely defeated as the fascism of Mussolini and Hitler. Still, however, it continued to provide the régimes that called themselves Marxist with a legitimacy that the fascist régimes could not summon to their aid. This is one of the paradoxes of the modern world.

By the second half of the twentieth century Marxism had acquired a foundation like that of Christianity or that of Mohammedanism. Half the intellectuals of the world called themselves Marxist and accepted, as a limiting framework for their own thinking, a sectarian tradition that bore the name, however much it may have departed from the teachings of Marx, which circumstances had shown to have been false. The paradox, here, corresponds to that of a Christianity which, in preaching and practice alike, departed at an early stage from what Christ himself taught—some of which (e.g., the prediction of the second coming in Matthew 24:34) was also betrayed by subsequent history. The consequence is that, identifying themselves nominally with an intellectual tradition now so well established and with such extensive philosophical roots, the communist régimes have thereby come to possess the peculiar psychological attribute called legitimacy, in the eyes of their own

people and half the rest of the world. With this support, none of them has been like the bicycle rider. None has needed to make war and to conquer in order to survive.

It is not easy to define what gives a body of doctrine power over the minds of men in the mass. Especially for those who are unlearned and have intellectual pretensions, a vague immensity of conception, a high level of abstraction, and obscurity of language seem to be essential. The clarity, the specificity, and the unequivocal language found in the writings of a Hobbes or a de Tocqueville can never move the world like the abstractions and obscurities of a Hegel, which permit a range of application and interpretation so wide that they can never be proved wrong. Hobbes required no exegesis, but the writers who have swayed the people have required whole libraries of it. Without the mystery that a Delphic ambiguity imparts, the limited minds of us poor mortals, forever seeking magic, cannot be satisfied. The unreadability of Marxist literature in general has contributed to its sway.

In any case, the fascist régimes, so predominantly adventuristic as they were, relying so exclusively on theatrical devices to maintain themselves in power, and scorning the uses of intellectuality true or false, were too superficial. They lacked the means to stabilize themselves.

The resemblances between the totalitarian dictatorships of the left and the totalitarian dictatorships of the right are very great. But the differences are fundamental.

29

ALL MOVEMENTS of right-wing radicalism have in common the impulse to restore a past, real or legendary, in which life was

simple, in which an austere morality prevailed, in which people accepted their respective places in a hierarchical order that represented nature's intention, and in which all were under the discipline of the common purpose to uphold this state of things. In this past, as taught to schoolchildren, the forefathers of the nation had shown an exemplary patriotism, not shrinking from the trials of war in the service of the national cause.

The two movements that we can, without equivocation, call fascist were extreme examples of this, involving the totalitarian organization of society and the mounting of theatrical spectacles. Mussolini's fascism looked back to the days of the Roman Empire, Hitler's National Socialism to a past over which the Norse gods had presided. While the early successes of Mussolini and Hitler still made it possible to regard them as worthy of imitation, Generalissimo Franco in Spain was inclined to imitate them; but with their downfall in World War II he reverted to something approaching the kind of conservative dictatorship that has commonly prevailed in countries lacking the cultural preconditions of liberal government. Elsewhere, as well, an occasional dictator assumed some of the trappings of fascism, only to discard them when it had been discredited by defeat in World War II.

The commonest type of right-wing radicalism since the war has been represented by such movements as that of McCarthyism in the United States and Poujadism in France. They appeal to simple people who, troubled by the increasing complexity and uncertainty of modern life, want to return to the security of the only world they regard as normal, the world remembered from childhood.

Representing the level of the common mind, these movements, like all ideological movements, are based on the fallacy of the two species. In the McCarthyist view of the world, which dominated the American mind in the nineteen-fifties, the members of a demonic species called communists were engaged in a

worldwide conspiracy to overthrow the order of society decreed by God and established by nature. In the United States these creatures had infiltrated the government, the universities, the churches, and the professions of mass communication to the point where they were on the verge of gaining complete control of the country. It followed that emergency measures were required to preserve the American way of life and American freedom. In the ensuing panic, free speech with respect to many key issues became too dangerous to practice, while thousands of honorable Americans, having suspicion cast on them, were persecuted, hounded, ruined in their careers, and forced to find whatever chink of obscurity they could in which to live out the times.

Such movements, varying in their extremism and prominence, exist in all countries where there is scope for diversity of opinion. They represent the reaction of frightened people to an accelerating change in the conditions of life that tends constantly to cast them adrift from their cultural moorings, from the sources of their psychological security in the remembered world of their childhood. While the basic cause is technological innovation, which tends to spread disorder by hastening the obsolescence of the customary order, it is abetted by the radicals of the left who deliberately promote disorder with the aim of destroying the society to which they stand in a relationship of alienation. What follows is that the animus of those who wish to preserve the society is directed against the left-wing radicals, regarded as an enemy species.

Radicalism of right and left alike leads to the police state and to its most damaging consequence, the suppression of the free discourse on which human progress ultimately depends. In this respect there is no choice to be made between the two radicalisms. However, in America and in other Western democracies, where the radicalism of the left is alien to the majority as the radicalism of the right is not, the left-wing extremists, by

promoting disorder, move the people to support the extremists of the right, who would be the ones to establish the succession in case of breakdown. We have the evidence of the contribution that left-wing militancy in Italy in the early nineteen-twenties, and in Germany in the early nineteen-thirties, made to the respective victories of fascism and National Socialism. Whatever weight one may attach to this evidence, and whatever conclusion one may draw from it, it still has its relevance to the question whether what follows the destruction of the established society should be of concern to those who pursue that end.

There is a balancing and a symmetry in all the realms of experience. According to the third law of mechanics, as Newton formulated it, "To every action there is always opposed an equal reaction...." The mounting threat of social disorder posed by accelerating change is identified with the intellectuals who promote it. Consequently, when people become sufficiently alarmed at the threat, they are impelled by their Hobbesian fears to welcome opposed movements that promise to maintain order by the forcible imposition of discipline. Such movements wear the aspect of conservatism because they represent the aim of returning to an idealized past in which the operations of society were simpler, traditional virtues were unquestioned, and any alien or subversive elements were kept in their place.

The situation is not essentially different in the twentieth century from what it was at the end of the fifth century B.C. in Greece. When Athens, having been defeated in the Peloponnesian War, fell into disorder, an anti-intellectual reaction set in, directed against any who had been subjecting the old beliefs and the old customs to the critical test of reason. The citizens of Athens, thinking they could thereby return to the lost past, put critical intelligence and free discourse to death in the person of Socrates.

30

Although Liberal societies are designed to accommodate diversity rather than to impose conformity, they still depend on what we call "a common mind" among the individuals who take part in their cultural and political life. The common mind provides the minimum cohesion that any society must have.

Common mind is the property of a society, but the term "society" itself embraces everything from mankind as a whole to the family household. There are concentric circles of society, overlapping societies, and within all large societies a variety of smaller ones. Some societies are formally organized and others, without formal organization, are identified only by affinity among individuals. Some are well defined, some vague. As there are divisions, subdivisions, and other complexes of society, and as there are various forms of society, so the phenomenon of a common mind manifests itself in corresponding complexes and forms.

Partisan manifestations of common mind are constantly forming with respect to particular and transient issues that divide any liberal society, so that, within the framework of a larger common mind, disagreement and debate between opposed groups take place. In a healthy society such conflict represents the Hegelian dialectic by which the common mind of the society as a whole progresses in knowledge and understanding.

The individual's active participation in a society is defined by the place he assumes in the complex of the common mind, with its divisions and subdivisions. His place is in some respects determined by birth—most persons, for example, being Protestant,

Catholic, or Jewish because they were born so. It may be determined by accidents of association: for example, the professional group in which an individual may, by fortuitous circumstances, find himself making his career. Finally, particular associations, connections, or sympathies may determine the common view that an individual shares on a particular issue.

To the extent that the individual identifies himself automatically with the common mind of any society or group he escapes the need to think for himself. What is more important, association with the common mind enables him to feel an assurance of being right that he could hardly feel otherwise. The fewest of us ever experience any doubt that "what we all say" must be true, that anything contrary to it must be false. In a world in which the best of us can know nothing for sure, this relieves us of the burden, not of our ignorance, which remains, but of the knowledge of our ignorance.

The assurance of his rightness that the individual derives from the common mind to which he has submitted his own is also an assurance of how wrong the members of another group, which takes an opposed position, are. Where assurance of this kind is greatest, the rightness of what is considered right and the wrongness of what is considered wrong seem so obvious that the disposition arises to attribute some kind of moral perversity to those who represent what is considered wrong. The extreme of such assurance is bigotry, and bigotry manifests itself in the Manichean distinction between the two species of every child's imagination, the good people and the bad.

The common mind, by its nature, is deficient in self-criticism. This can be seen and demonstrated, I think, even on the smallest scale. I have known meetings of individuals, every one exceptional in knowledge and intelligence, to agree unanimously on a false proposition that no one of them, thinking for himself, would have accepted. In such circumstances, each commonly supposes that, since all the others accept the proposition, it must

be right. Any doubts he may still experience he answers, in the privacy of his own mind, by an uneasy supposition that he must have missed some consideration which the others had grasped. Add to this that he would risk discredit or hostility if he dissented from what everyone else accepted.

I would maintain that the highest intellectual distinction is manifested only by the individual mind that thinks for itself. Thinking for itself, however, and expressing its thought freely, the individual mind, even under the best of circumstances, is bound to incur the hostility and, in whatever degree, the persecution of the common mind.

The opposition of society to the freedom of the individual mind takes different forms in different circumstances. It took one form in Athens in 399 B.C. In Galileo's Italy it took a form not dissimilar to what it takes in Russia or China today. In our liberal societies, where tolerance of dissent has traditionally been accounted a virtue, it has become intensified, as we shall see, by the increase in the number of people who participate in political and cultural activity.

31

INCREASE IN THE number of persons participating together in any activity that calls for intellectual or cultural refinement tends toward the predominance of mediocrity. Such increase is one of the features of our times. It is, in part, the consequence of the absolute increase of population, in part of the secular development whereby an increasing proportion of the increasing population is active in political and cultural concerns. Never before have there been national societies numbering hundreds of millions, or cities of ten million. Never before have academic

communities been so large; never before have the scholars in every major field of inquiry numbered in the tens of thousands. By far the majority of those who have ever written history are writing it today, and if what is true of history is not true of all academic pursuits the exceptions would be hard to find.

In the most developed countries today, participation in political debate and struggle is no longer confined to a minority. Newspapers formerly designed to appeal to the few now compete in appealing to the millions. Increasingly, debate on the political issues of the day is formulated in terms suitable for transmission by the newly developed media of mass communication.

One effect of mass participation in political debate is the increasing tendency for such debate to be carried on by demonstration in the streets, where the views of opposing partisans can be expressed only in such slogans as may be shouted in unison or printed on placards. This represents a falling off from the highest standard of public debate, as exemplified by the series of articles, collectively known as *The Federalist*, which appeared in the American press in 1787 and 1788. By excluding those processes of thoughtful deliberation for which the individual mind is best fitted, such means of carrying on political contests allow only bigotry.

I have mentioned that the great majority of those who have ever written history are writing it today. To estimate that, in the middle of the eighteenth century, as many as twenty persons were writing history in English may be to exaggerate, but the order of magnitude is all that matters here. In 1970, the membership of the American Historical Association was about 17,000, that of The Historical Association in Britain about 12,000. The total of 29,000 omits many historians using the English language in countries other than the United States and Britain, but it also includes many persons interested in historical scholarship who are not themselves engaged in writing history. It seems safe to

estimate that about 1970 there were at least 15,000 historians writing history in English.[1] Of the twenty in the eighteenth century, at least two, Gibbon and Hume, were men of intellectual distinction, cultivated in wisdom. We may be sure that, in the case of the 15,000, the rate is not as high, that it is not 10 per cent, that the men of like distinction do not come to 1,500.

Whatever social pressures Gibbon was under in writing his history, he was not under pressure from other historians of his day associated together as a professional community. Where historians number only twenty there are no such reasons for professional association as where they number fifteen thousand. One reason for such association when the number rises so high is a proper concern for agreeing upon standards of procedure and presentation in the practice of history. An individual of intellect and cultivation will hardly need to be told to make sure that the sources of his information are reliable or that he should look at all sides of any issue he chronicles. Where history is a mass undertaking, however, one cannot assume intellect and cultivation in its practitioners. The consequence is that, in all the social sciences, the swelling of numbers has been accompanied by an increasing preoccupation with methodology (a word more calculated to impress than "method").

Large-scale professional associations are bound to be concerned, as well, with the protection or advancement of narrower common interests. One form this takes is the cultivation of a distinction between "insiders" and "outsiders," and here something like the trade-union spirit may come to manifest itself. Insiders are recognized as such if they have an academic degree showing that they have undergone a course of training that is likely to be, in part, a course of indoctrination in orthodoxy, in

---

[1] The explosive character of the growth involved here, as in so many other domains, is indicated by the following figures on the membership of the American Historical Association (information kindly given in a letter to the author on August 18, 1970, from Miss E. M. Gaylard of the A.M.H.): in 1884, 40; in 1900, about 500; in 1955, 5,400; in 1967, 15,600; and in 1970, approximately 17,000.

attitudes of mind, in conventional judgments, and in the technical language, obscure to outsiders, by which the insiders recognize one another. It is not irrelevant that this language involves a sacrifice of clarity in expression which the distinguished individual will be moved to resist.

To the degree that a professional association numbering thousands is a self-serving association, the interests it serves are those of the undistinguished majority. That majority determines the common mind of the whole, and another Hobbes, another Gibbon, or another de Tocqueville will find himself under pressure to abnegate his distinction, to conform, to adopt the ways and the jargon of the majority. It he does not meet the qualifications it has established, however tacitly, for acceptance as an insider, he will be faced by special difficulties. If he is markedly nonconformist, the word will go around professional circles that he is not "sound," and the director of any academic organization to which he is attached may be approached confidentially by colleagues who feel the obligation of calling attention to his lack of qualification, if not for continued employment, then for advancement. He may find that he is denied publication for what he writes, since the editors of learned journals represent the professional establishment, while even commercial publishers of books must consult the view of the establishment before deciding whether to accept or reject any manuscript he submits. If he succeeds in getting his books published anyway, he will hardly be able to count on the sympathy of the professionals who review them.

To be fair, I must call attention to how easily these difficulties may be exaggerated by mere statement. All is a matter of degree here, and the tolerance accorded outsiders varies with cases and circumstances. Most of us could, however, cite instances that show the danger which arises when the common mind comes, by increasing numbers, increasingly to outweigh the distinguished individual mind. I recall an occasion when a thesis submitted for

the Ph.D., which the jury reluctantly recognized as brilliant, original, and true, was almost condemned because, as one juror said, it was "not political science." De Tocqueville's *Democracy in America*, which also is not political science, would surely have been turned down.

The tyranny of the common mind, with its inherent mediocrity, is the agency that, in our own times as in the Athens of 399 B.C., persecutes the individual distinction on which mankind depends for its progress. The tyranny of the common mind is, in turn, a product of increasing mass participation in all social and cultural activity, which is a feature of our own times as of Athens twenty-four centuries ago.

The relevance of this to the subject of these pages is that ideological thinking is the kind of thinking native to the common mind.

32

IN CHAPTER I I adopted a narrow definition of "ideology," confining the term to "bodies of doctrine that present themselves as affording systems of belief so complete that whole populations may live by them alone. . . ." At the end of the last chapter I referred to "ideological thinking," a term that denotes a habit of mind rather than a body of doctrine. The application to society of any abstract principle assumed to have the status of moral law, as if representing the intention of God or nature, is what I mean here by "ideological thinking." Ideological thinking, whether right or wrong, is normative thinking so sure of its own rightness as to be intolerant of dissent. For purposes of the discussion here, it makes no difference whether it does or does not embrace a complete system of belief.

In his Introduction to *Democracy in America,* written in 1831, de Tocqueville, observing that the drive of Christian society since the eleventh century had been toward universal social equality, went on to predict that, for better or worse, it would continue until it had somehow fulfilled itself.

The history that has since transpired has confirmed this prediction. Slavery has been abolished; the association of privilege with birth has been largely eliminated, as has discrimination on grounds of race or color; educational opportunities have increasingly been made available to all; universal adult suffrage has become established, and lately the tendency has been to lower the age at which it may be enjoyed. The same drive was manifested toward the end of the nineteen-sixties by the demand of university students for administrative and pedagogical reforms that would reduce the inequality of status and power between them, on the one hand, and their teachers and the university administrators on the other. In the international sphere, the principle of the equality of all nations, large and small, has been given the standing of international law by inclusion in the Charter of United Nations.

It is not too much to say that, by the second half of the twentieth century, the abstract principle of human equality had acquired, throughout the world, the status of a moral law, not to be questioned, and the drive for the elimination of the last exceptions to its realization in practice was being charged with increasing passion.[1]

In the spring of 1970, at a meeting in Washington of the Democratic Party's Committee on National Priorities, Dr. Edgar F. Berman, a physician, addressing himself to the issue of equal opportunity for women, "argued that physical factors, particularly the menstrual cycle and menopause, disqualified

---

[1] The dynamics that account for the increasing passion, as the goal of total equality is ever more closely approached, is explained in de Tocqueville, Vol. I, Chap. IV, p. 56.

women for key executive jobs."[1] He said that these factors might impair a woman's judgment at a time when a crucial decision had to be taken. This aroused the indignation of Representative Patsy T. Mink of Hawaii, who wrote to the head of the Democratic Party, Hubert H. Humphrey, demanding that he seek Dr. Berman's resignation from the Committee. "I am certain," she wrote, "you will be appalled at Dr. Berman's disgusting performance in which he displayed the basest sort of prejudice against women, characterizing us as mentally incapable to govern, let alone aspire to equality, because we are physiologically inferior." Faced with the moral outrage his remarks had aroused, Dr. Berman tried to defend himself but ended by resigning from the Committee in public disgrace.

As a man professionally concerned with facts rather than ideology, Dr. Berman had imprudently given his medical opinion on a question of fact. But the question that presented itself to Representative Mink's mind was one of ideology. So far from challenging his allegation of fact, her reference to women as "physiologically inferior" could be regarded as accepting and even going beyond it. One gathers that in her view, and perhaps quite rightly, the ideological principle should prevail, even at such cost as might be imposed by the factual situation. In any case, this incident is an example of conflict between empirical thinking, on the one hand, and, on the other, normative thinking that meets our definition of ideological thinking by its intolerance of questioning.

I have illustrated ideological thinking by the principle of equality because it is the dominant social principle of modern times. It represents, as no other principle does, our common sense of justice. However, as the movement to realize it in practice, which de Tocqueville traced back to the eleventh century, approaches fulfillment, the disparity and tension that always exist between the normative world of our minds and the world of

[1] *International Herald-Tribune*, Paris, July 26, 1970.

factual circumstances take on dimensions that may prove tragic.

The disparity and tension may be illustrated by the constant extension of voting rights in our democracies. Their original confinement to the small portion of the population that belonged to the male sex, owned land, and represented high levels of education, was relaxed until the entire population over the age of twenty was included. By the continuing process of widening the application of the principle, the minimum age is now being lowered, here and there, to eighteen. If this minimum age should continue to be lowered progressively, a point would come, sooner for some and later for others, where it would seem unrealistic to carry the process further. I cite this hypothetical situation simply to indicate that a point could be reached at which the most extreme ideologist would not be so doctrinaire as to advocate that the application of the principle of equality be carried any further.

In actual experience it may be that an optimum point, in terms of workability, has been passed well before the point is reached at which any further application would be obviously absurd. Democracy, as it evolves in particular societies, tends to run a course that rises to an optimum, from which it then declines into increasing irresponsibility and ultimate chaos. The Athenian assembly, including all the citizens of Athens, was originally subordinate to a king, to aristocratic archons, and to the aristocratic council of the Areopagus. Over four or five centuries, however, the independent powers of the aristocratic elements declined as the power of the assembly increased until, in the time of Pericles, the assembly at last became absolute. After Pericles, the mass democracy that had developed so naturally proved increasingly incapable of coping with the complex and delicate problems that the state had to resolve. Self-serving demagogues rose to power, and decisions were taken increasingly under the influence of the mob spirit they

evoked and fostered, until all ended in the disaster so movingly related by Thucydides.

Earlier I had occasion to remark on how deliberative debate, as the process of reaching decision, appears to be giving way to street demonstrations in the great democracies of our own day. Under such circumstances, ideological thinking becomes more prominent. It was on ideological grounds that the Athenian assembly, representing a relatively low average of intellectual understanding, condemned and sentenced Socrates.

33

IDEOLOGICAL thinking, defined as I have defined it, may be inimical to the making of responsible decisions. By responsible decisions I mean decisions that take the fullest possible account of consequences.

The commonest weakness of left-wing radicalism, as we have seen, has been its disposition to assume that the destruction of an existing system of society in its entirety will necessarily be followed by something better. What the representatives of such radicalism have in mind as something better, however, is never what actually follows. What followed the destruction of the French monarchy was the Terror and Bonapartism. What followed the overthrow of the czarist régime was Stalinism. What followed the destruction of the Weimar Republic, in which the left-wing radicals played a decisive part, was Hitlerism.

Engels, who in his later years became increasingly cynical about Marxists and revolutionaries generally, wrote in 1885 to Vera Zasulich, one of the founders of the Russian Marxist movement:

Supposing these people [the revolutionaries] imagine they can seize power, what does it matter? Provided they make the hole which will shatter the dyke [dike], the flood itself will soon rob them of their illusions. But if by chance these illusions resulted in giving them a superior force of will, why complain of that? People who boasted that they had made a revolution have always seen the next day that they had no idea what they were doing, that the revolution made did not in the least resemble the one they would have liked to make.[1]

Lenin, long before he died, could have confirmed the last sentence quoted above. Hitler, in the years leading up to 1933, might well have written the first two.

Because left-wing radicalism, by contrast with that of the right, is intellectual, it appeals chiefly to the groups we lump together as "intellectuals": academics, writers, artists, and those in allied pursuits. The intellectuals have come to constitute an important class in our modern societies, a sort of ideological priesthood. The class as a whole, through the phenomenon of the common mind, tends to take positions on the great issues that confront national and international society, each member typically accepting for himself the conclusions of its common mind. But, as is always the case, its common mind has been formed by the exclusion of individual distinction, which is always disrupting to the formation of a common mind.

When national or international populations of intellectuals have risen into the hundreds of thousands we may be sure that the mass of them have special intellectual qualifications more by aspiration than by accomplishment. Wishing to identify themselves with the class that seems to represent intellectual authority, and to be accepted in it, they are the more ready to adopt its intellectual attitudes and repeat its intellectual formulations.

We must take account, I think, of a general intellectual debasement that is the consequence of increased numbers, of specialization, and of an attitude hostile to the distinction that

[1] Marx and Engels, 1934, p. 437.

tends to disrupt consensus. Many persons, although they have acquired advanced degrees like the Ph.D. by mastering some specialized subject, lack a high general education and may even be unable to write or speak good English. The expansion of university teaching staffs has entailed a deterioration in the qualifications of the teachers as well as a general lowering of educational standards.[1]

I am groping, here, for the explanation of why it is that the intellectual class, which has shown itself uniquely vulnerable to the appeal of left-wing radicalism, has not been more resistant to the irresponsibility represented by a drive for destruction that is so careless of consequences. Part of the explanation, surely, is that intellectuals, in so far as their preoccupation is with nominal abstractions, judge political and social movements not by what they actually do but by their labels and the attitudes they proclaim. This, I take it, is why, for almost a generation, so many high-minded intellectuals regarded Stalin as another Abraham Lincoln, committing themselves to his intellectual leadership on the grounds that he represented the realization of Marx's prophecy. The nominal was more real for them than the real.

We cannot, I think, understand the record of the intellectuals since 1917 unless we understand how naive and even unworldly the rank and file may be. I am not the only one who, as a former foreign-office official, has been surprised to learn that it is easier to discuss the issues of international relations with a group of businessmen than with the members of a university faculty. The reason is that every issue that presents itself to a government for

---

[1] A professor of law at the University of Michigan, interviewed by a magazine on the subject of threats to the individual's privacy, made the following statement: "The individual is being informationally raped. The government, credit bureaus, the police and others have their fangs in this guy. They each have their piece of information about this guy, and he doesn't have access to the information." (*Newsweek*, July 27, 1970, p. 25.) Thought at a high level is not possible in language like this. The informational material sent out even by some of the best American universities today is often written in the English of the uneducated.

resolution is likely, in its reality, to constitute an intricate problem that has no clear and unequivocal solution, which is something that businessmen are familiar with from their own experience. To the rank and file of intellectuals, however, who think ideologically, the same issues are apt to appear as simple issues of right or wrong, issues that do not have valid arguments on both sides. It is significant that on such issues as arouse public passion, like the American government's decision to intervene in Cambodia in May 1970, free discussion may not be possible on university campuses, where only one position is tolerated, while it continues elsewhere.

In the fall of 1956 I attended a meeting of professional intellectuals from many countries. Great Britain and France, at the time, had just committed the disastrous blunder of an armed intervention to regain control of the Suez Canal, after its seizure by the Egyptian government. The members of the meeting were apparently unanimous in their indignation at the Anglo-French move. One member after another arose to "testify," as at a revival meeting, sometimes testifying in the name of the intellectuals of his country, sometimes even in the name of his country's people. Having recently come from years of service in a foreign office, I had not caught the spirit of the occasion, and unfortunate circumstances led me into indiscretion. It was only after I had arrived at the meeting and had picked up a copy of the program that I had found myself billed on it as one of the two principal speakers, and since I had not been told that I would be expected to speak I had prepared nothing. When the time came, then, I was moved to rectify what seemed to me an imbalance in the preceding discussion. Without pretending that the Franco-British action had been justified, I called attention to the practical threat that, as I saw it, the seizure of the canal posed. I pointed out that the West European countries depended on the canal for the imports of petroleum and petroleum products on which their economies depended, so

that if the Egyptian government should use its newly won power to close the canal the economic life of West Europe might be strangled, with consequences alarming to contemplate.

I still suffer from the memory of the reaction to my remarks, which I shall not describe. All was summed up in the statement of one speaker that, as intellectuals, the members of the meeting were properly concerned only with ideological issues, that economic problems and such questions as the supply of oil should properly be left for the people in foreign offices to deal with.

This seemed to me deeply irresponsible at the time, and after the lapse of so many years it still does. It assumes that questions of what policies a society should adopt and what actions it should take may properly be answered on ideological grounds without regard for practical consequences.

The reader will see the connection between this indifference to consequences and the experience of the Bolshevik intellectuals after they had seized power, as described by Radek in the interview cited in the last footnote of Chapter 23. It is this indifference, also, that allows so many left-wing intellectuals to promote the disorder that, if they should be successful, could only have the effect of bringing the radicals of the right into power.

34

A PRINCIPLE of personal conduct that represents the common mind of intellectuals in our time is that of commitment. Rather than standing apart from the social struggles of our day, each of us should enter the fray by committing himself. Commitment, in addition to being a duty, is regarded as justifying itself in what it does for the individual. As certain French writers have put it, it is essential to the "authentic" life.

The fact that the question of what one should commit oneself to is not ordinarily raised, in advancing the principle of commitment, suggests either that it does not arise or that it presents no difficulty. What, in fact, is the explanation of such indifference to a question so central?

It is clear that the advocates of commitment are not really indifferent to what an individual commits himself to, that they would not approve of commitment, for instance, to fascism or to the re-establishment of Negro slavery. If, then, they neglect the question, it must be because they assume that it is always obvious, in social conflict, which is the good side and which the bad, and it goes without saying that one should commit oneself to the good—or, as they are more apt to think of it, that one should commit oneself to fight the bad. What is fundamental here is Manicheism, the fallacy of the two species, the assumption every child makes that the world is divided between the good people and the bad. Implicit in Manicheism, moreover, is Pharisaism, for the good people are ourselves.

The record of the committed intellectuals, however, itself shows that the world is not this simple. Again I cite their allegiance over the years to Stalin and his intellectual leadership, up to the time when the word went out that he was not one of the good people after all, but one of the bad.

If we judge by Mr. Jean-Paul Sartre, who is the most prominent advocate of commitment today, commitment *against* appears to present fewer difficulties of choice than commitment *for*. In the French underground resistance during the Second World War he opposed the Nazis who had conquered and occupied his country. One can understand the exhilarating sense he must have had during those years of living an authentic life. After the war, one supposes, a replacement for the Nazis was needed if the authentic life was to be continued. The replacement was an abstraction called "the bourgeoisie," the old mythological monster of Karl Marx's creative imagination. It took the form of

something called "bourgeois society," especially as represented by the governing establishment in his native France. For purposes of his opposition to the bourgeoisie, then, he made common cause with the Stalinists, breaking with them only when they had become so discredited that one could hardly continue to deal with them as if they were the good people. His commitment, it transpired, had not been *for* Stalinism but *against* bourgeois society. We know, then, what he has been *against*, but if he has been *for* anything we do not know what. We do not know what he would put in the place of the bourgeois state.

I cite this case because it illustrates my thesis that the left-wing commitment to destruction is irresponsible in so far as it is indifferent to what may follow its accomplishment. The destruction of the Weimar Republic, in which the generation of left-wing intellectuals before Mr. Sartre's participated, was followed by Hitler's totalitarian state. Can we be sure that the destruction of the Fifth Republic would not be followed by something as bad? Surely the therapeutic value of commitment to battle, the sense it gives the individual of leading an authentic life, is not enough to justify such indifference to consequences.

Students who have participated in the student revolutionary movements that began in the second half of the nineteen-sixties have told me, in justification of those movements, how exalted they felt as they marched shoulder to shoulder with their fellow students against the barricades. For the moment they were living the authentic life. There was the escape from the loneliness and weakness that are the lot of the individual as such. Moving and shouting in unison with the mob, they felt themselves part of an invincible moral rectitude that was realizing itself with irresistible power.

I do not doubt that the Hitler Jugend of an earlier generation, marching past their Führer with arms raised in salute, enjoyed the same exhilaration. For them, too, the authentic life was being realized. In the one case no less than in the other, however, one

must ask whether the therapeutic benefits are worth the consequences.

Modern ideologies and the simplicities of ideological thinking have developed to meet the needs of societies based on the conception of popular sovereignty and the general will. Their function is to make the people one in thought and action, to make them singular rather than plural. Their function is to displace the mind that thinks for itself, to afford the comfort of certainty where there is no certainty, to eliminate questioning. The immediate benefits they confer are great, and it is only the ultimate consequences that have to be feared.

35

"On no other account do I congratulate myself more," said Erasmus, "than on the fact that I have never attached myself to any party."[1]

It is evident that the burden of freedom and the requirements of intellectual responsibility are too great for most of us to bear. On the other hand, the service of truth and the realization of mankind's possibilities require that a Socrates, a Boethius, an Erasmus, a Galileo, a Voltaire, a Darwin, or an Einstein be able to practice a measure of independence from the accepted thinking of official establishments or of that alternative oppressor, the common mind. A balance must be kept which permits the survival of the individual mind that, thinking for itself, questions, and because it questions, dissents.

The common mind is indispensable to the functioning of any liberal society, for without it there would be social chaos, which

[1] Huizinga, pp. 135–136.

could be resolved only by a police dictatorship. The common mind is also necessary to the great majority that depend on it for their inner happiness. The members of a society must therefore be brought up to a set of common norms that arise out of its traditions, are represented by its classics of literature, art, and music, and are communicated through a common educational system. To use Hegel's word for it, they must be brought up to a common *Sittlichkeit*.

While some norms are surely valid for all times and all places, secular change tends in time to invalidate most, so that they tend to be constantly obsolescent. It follows that they must undergo constant adaptation and transformation over the generations. Norms of thought and behavior that suited the predominantly agricultural society of Jefferson's day do not suit the industrial and urban society that has taken its place. The principal reasons for allowing the individual mind to function freely is for its contribution to the necessary process of adaptation and transformation. When the progress of knowledge has made the first chapter of Genesis obsolete, a Darwin must not be prevented from advancing beyond it.

The problem today is that the constant acceleration of change has reached a point at which the adaptation of traditional norms, if it is to keep pace, must be so rapid as to entail, increasingly, the breaking of the continuity by which they have hitherto kept their connection with tradition. At the same time, increasing mass participation in forming public taste, in setting standards of behavior, and in determining the directions taken by our great national societies gives an ever greater role to barbarism and intolerance. The extremism of ideological thinking becomes increasingly the rule, and rival ideological groups carry their conflicts into the streets.

It is not clear to me that, when the common mind acquires a mass basis, there is as much to choose between one faction and another as one might wish. Bigotry is abhorrent in itself, what-

ever the cause with which it is associated. The stark fact is that, by 1970, free speech on the issue of the Indo-Chinese War was still possible virtually everywhere in the United States except on university campuses. The vast intellectual communities of modern times are, as we have seen, more vulnerable than others to ideological thinking, with its intolerance.

As one who has learned to comfort himself with the thought that what generally happens in history is the unexpected, I do not predict anything as specific as the collapse of civilization. Disorder, however, there will surely be. My concern is that throughout the disorder, whatever form it takes and however long it lasts, the human spirit at its best and the possibilities of eventually resuming human progress be preserved. The two go together.

Let me deal first with the human spirit at its best. "Take a man by himself," said George Gissing's Henry Ryecroft,

> and there is generally some reason to be found in him, some disposition for good; mass him with his fellows in the social organism, and ten to one he becomes a blatant creature, without a thought of his own, ready for any evil to which contagion prompts him. It is because nations tend to stupidity and baseness that mankind moves so slowly; it is because individuals have a capacity for better things that it moves at all.[1]

If the God of the Old Testament should threaten mankind with another flood, and if it were my duty to put the case for mankind before him, I would first of all point to its progress since the days when men were like the other anthropoids that lived in the darkness of the forests. It would not be its material progress that I would point to, however. I would, rather, point to Homer's *Odyssey*, to *The Trojan Women* of Euripides, to Plato's *Apology*, to the great tragedies of Shakespeare, to Melville's *Moby Dick*, to Lincoln's Second Inaugural Address,

---

[1] Gissing, Book I ("Spring"), Chap. 16, p. 48.

to James Elroy Flecker's *Hassan,* to Thornton Wilder's *Bridge of San Luis Rey*; I would point to the masses and cantatas of Johann Sebastian Bach, to Mozart's *Coronation Mass,* and to Bruch's *Kol Nidrei*; I would point to the Aphrodite of Melos, to Michelangelo's frescoes on the ceiling of the Sistine Chapel and to his "Pietá"; I would point to the integrity of Socrates, of Boethius, of Thomas More, and of Milovan Djilas. I would point to the fact that mankind's vision of the universe in which it finds itself has been progressively enlarged in the successive visions associated with the names of Ptolemy, Newton, and Einstein. In every case, and without deciding to do so in advance, what I pointed out as a reason for sparing mankind would be associated primarily with one individual, and only secondarily with the society to which he belonged.[1] I would not say: look at ancient Greece, look at Renaissance Italy, look at Elizabethan England, look at eighteenth-century France, look at Jefferson's America. All these were sordid and pitiful societies except as they were exalted by the virtue of a few individuals.

Let me add that I have sometimes thought, while listening to Rostropovich on the cello, to Menuhin on the violin, or to Maria Stader singing, that, if there were a personal God who heard the appeal, because of it alone he would spare mankind the miseries that are in store for it. It is achievements like these that would justify the redemption of mankind.

What a long way we have come toward the light, after all, since we lived like apes in the dark forest! If what we wish is to continue this progress, should not our intellectual and moral leaders, rather than succumbing to mass bigotry, be concerned with how to keep the door open for its continuance?

What, then, are the requirements for keeping the door open?

---

[1] "Primarily with one individual," but secondarily with the society, because, as Hegel put it, "all great men have formed themselves in solitude, but only by working for themselves upon what the state [i.e., society, in his usage] had already created." In Kaufmann, 1966, p. 269.

36

I F WHAT IS BEST in mankind, and what its progress depends on, manifests itself primarily in the individual and only secondarily in the mass, then our objective should be to maintain such freedom as allows the individual to think and speak for himself. This does not depend only on institutional safeguards, like those included in the Constitution of the United States, for we have seen how, when McCarthysim was dominant in the early nineteen-fifties, and when bigotry again came into the ascendent at the end of the nineteen-sixties (at least in the universities) social pressures associated with ideological thinking alone sufficed to stifle such freedom. Toleration of dissent depends, rather, on certain conceptual preconditions in the minds of men.

The basic precondition is an appreciation of our own ignorance. We have to recognize that, on virtually any point at all, the most knowledgeable of us may be wrong. Here, however, we confront a psychological impulse common to us all. We are unwilling to face the fact of the unknown because it fills us with fear or imposes on us the strain of a perplexing uncertainty. Therefore, although an individual may recognize his own ignorance, he is comforted by the assumption that there are others who know what he does not, just as a small child is comforted by the assumption that there is nothing his parents do not know. Perhaps the individual, of himself, does not know why he is on earth and what the purpose of existence is, but he can go to a priest who can tell him. Although he, of himself, does not know the reason for a pain in his body, he has access to a doctor who does know about such things. The reason for the aurora borealis may be a mystery to him personally, but it does not

disturb him as long as he has no doubt that there are men of science who understand it.

It is as if all mankind were engaged in a conspiracy to cover up the fact of its ignorance. For the doctor does not let his patient see how little he actually does know, the priest does not turn a member of his flock away with the answer that he has no answer, the professor does not reject the authority that those who sit at his feet attribute to him, a prophet like Karl Marx does not announce that he may be wrong about the future, and the President of the United States does not tell the American people that he is at a loss to know how to deal with the problems that confront the nation. It is part of the tragedy of humankind that this pretence must be maintained over the whole wide scene of human concerns. And those who engage in it are generally a, much misled by it as those at whom it is directed. One who is himself a professor may be allowed to observe that few professors, after years of giving answers *ex cathedra* to students who are not qualified to challenge them, have much sense of their own ignorance left. At last, even where every other authority has been discredited, there is the conviction that what we all say must be true because we all say it.

Before the French Revolution, when society was organized on an hierarchical basis, the mass of men, illiterate as well as ignorant, took it for granted that their "betters" knew what they themselves did not, and this has persisted to our own day in the belief that one man, an Eisenhower or a Mao Tse-tung, knows. However, with the increasing realization of egalitarianism, all such authority has tended to be eroded, to the point where we can today recognize the development of a crisis of authority in the advanced countries of the world. Parents have less authority over their children, teachers have less authority over students, the Pope has less authority over the priesthood, and governments have less authority over the governed. All that is left, at last, in the egalitarian society is the authority of the common

mind, an authority that has its origin in a common ignorance decked out with the ostentation of knowledge.

All of us develop the skill, in discussion, of dissembling our ignorance. Among those of us with the least cultivation, the least intelligence, and the least knowledge, the custom is to compete in false displays of special knowledge. Listen to the conversation of young bucks gathered together on a street corner anywhere and one is likely to pick up such rare bits of information as what the President of the United States has secretly in mind, or what the communists are really up to in Vietnam.

On the other hand, the more highly developed a man's mind and education, the more he will recognize how hard it is to be sure of anything. A man who has made a lifelong study of China will find it harder to know what is going on there than the young buck on the street corner.

Only the most knowledgeable know how little is known for sure, or at all, even after the long centuries in which we have been accumulating knowledge. The increase of specialization in recent times has, moreover, made it more difficult to be knowledgeable enough to know how little is known. Although a wise doctor may be aware of how much remains unknown to the medical profession, he may well assume that the advanced economists of his day have at last arrived at a full understanding of the economic problems of mankind. An equally wise economist will know better, but may, in turn, assume that the basic way in which biological evolution works is known, although a wise biologist will know better. The layman knows that Newton was wrong in his explanation of the universe, but he supposes that the right answer has now been given by Einstein.

All of us are brought up on the distinction between "what people used to believe" and "what we now know." We may well expect, however, that, if human progress continues, "what we now know" will come to be regarded as "what people used to believe."

If our knowledge of the physical world is incomplete, our understanding of politics hardly exists at all, for politics is one aspect of human nature in action, and human nature eludes us. Yet this is the realm in which ideological thinking is most prevalent, in which the self-assurance of the bigoted is greatest.

It is recognition of the fact that no man or group of men has possession of ultimate truth, that at best only partial, contingent, and tentative truths, mixed with error, are available to any of us, that is the basis for the tolerance of diversity on which our liberal societies were founded. Those societies had their origin in the age of skepticism, when Western civilization developed the critical faculty that was necessary for the recognition of human ignorance.

37

Newton's view of the universe was true in substantial part and with respect to a limited range of phenomena, but it left much out of account and contained an important admixture of error. Einstein's view, which corrects it, takes more into account and eliminates some of the error. What we know of the truth, however, is still partial, still relative, and still mixed with error. The questions about the universe that remain unanswered still dwarf what we have come to know. This is the nature of such truth as we men have been able to master. It follows that we must not confine our thinking to the categorical terms "true" and "false." What we know is, at best, partly true within limits.

> Both in science and in logic [Whitehead wrote], you have only to develop your argument sufficiently, and sooner or later you are bound to arrive at a contradiction, either internally within the argument, or externally in its reference to fact. . . . None of these logical or scientific myths is wrong, in an unqualified sense of that term. It is unguarded. Its truth is limited by unexpressed

presuppositions; and as time goes on, we discover some of these limitations. The simple-minded use of the notions "right or wrong" is one of the chief obstacles to the progress of understanding.[1]

How does the incompleteness of all truth bear on the question of tolerance, which is our theme here?

"The fact is," Reinhold Niebuhr has written, "that any commitment, religious, political, or cultural, can lead to intolerance if there is not a certain degree of residual awareness of the possibility of error in the truth in which we believe, and of the possibility of truth in the error against which we contend."[2] To turn this statement around, tolerance depends on such awareness.

If I believed that there was anyone to whom final truth was known, or that such truth was in any doctrine, then I would not believe in tolerance; for any departure from the unquestionable truth would be unquestionable error, and there would be no justification for tolerating it. I believe in tolerance only because the one thing I feel sure of is our common ignorance. There have been no gods among us, and no prophets possessed of a more than human insight. When it comes to knowing what is right in any ultimate sense, or knowing the destination of history, or knowing what course men should follow in obedience to some authority greater than their own, or knowing what life means, I know as much as Moses, St. Paul, Mahomet, Hobbes, Rousseau, Hegel, Marx, or Mao Tse-tung. Yet I have no absolute knowledge beyond the fact that *cogito, ergo sum.* The "knowledge" I have beyond that consists, at best, merely of intimations of truth more or less convincing, more or less applicable to my experience.

Such knowledge short of the absolute, however, is constantly being increased through the free operation among us of the dialectical process by which every statement leads to question-

---

[1] In Kaufmann, 1966, p. 170.
[2] Niebuhr, p. 352.

ing that leads to its modification or replacement. The progress we thus make is borne out by our experience. Except in terms of such absolute knowledge as is limited to *cogito, ergo sum,* I am less ignorant than Moses or Marx because I know that the universe is at least 10^{23} kilometers across (a distance that light, moving at 300,000 km. per second, takes some ten million years to travel); I know that the number of the stars is at least many hundreds of millions of millions, and that a considerable proportion of these are sufficiently like our sun so that one may plausibly expect some millions of them, at least, to be accompanied by planets on which life has developed. I also know that our own little planet, this mote in space, must have had life on it for some four thousand million years.

All this knowledge makes what Moses thought obsolete. It tends to make obsolete any view of the world, like Hegel's, in which all being exists only for the sake of our own species, here on earth, which is regarded as occupying the central position in the cosmos.[1]

We have also made progress in the knowledge of our own kind since the days when it was possible for Aristotle to believe that man was an animal whose nature it was to live in city-states, or since Dante believed that there was a God who, having created all being, intended that all mankind, the crown of all being, should be under the government of the Holy Roman Emperor (the crown of the crown of all being). We have made progress since the days when it was possible for Marx to believe that all history was the history of class struggle, and that all history in this

---

[1] Ontological thinking appears not to have caught up with the implications either of evolution or cosmology. Even if this earth were all, there would be no reason to regard our species as the final end of evolution. (What evolutionary theory reveals is that all life is one, not divided between man and all other beings as we had thought.) The self-centered humanism of existentialists and of such visionaries as Teilhard de Chardin, however, almost depends on ignorance of the cosmos that the cosmologists have come to know. The reason for the ignorance may be the general repugnance among humanist intellectuals for anything that has to do with the exploration of space. The repugnance, in turn, reflects humanism.

sense was about to come to an end with the final elimination of classes.

Yet all we know today, unimaginable as much of it would have been even to Newton or Darwin, let alone to Moses or Aristotle —all we know is as nothing alongside all we do not know. When it comes to the matters with which ideologies deal, the ignorance of the best among us is still virtually total.

If we recognize that mankind has never achieved more than partial and relative truths, mixed with error, and if we believe that the quest for truth is far from an end, that it is continuing and progressive, and that it requires a constant purification and enlargement of such truth as we already know by the correction of error, then we shall consider it essential to allow the process by which truth is purified and enlarged, and by which error is corrected, to continue. We shall consider it essential to provide for the continuance of the process by which every argument, exposed for criticism and correction, is thereby replaced by a modified or alternative argument that, in its turn, is exposed for criticism and correction. Criticism and correction can hardly operate, however, where an official establishment with a monopoly of power forbids them, or where they are forbidden by a common mind which, in its ignorance and simplicity, believes that, since what it regards as truth is unquestionable, any questioning of it must *ipso facto* serve the cause of error.

The skeptics and empiricists of the seventeenth and eighteenth centuries, like Locke and Voltaire, favored tolerance because they knew that, the questionability of human knowledge being what it is, all interdiction of questioning could serve only to preserve and perpetuate half-truths and falsehood.

The masses of people in the seventeenth and eighteenth centuries would not have had the cultivated understanding necessary to appreciate the fact that bigotry must always be on the side of falsehood. The masses of people in our own time, with a relatively higher level of education, still lack such understand-

ing. The evidence of the past few decades indicates that even university communities, with the highest education of all, lack it. The explanation is, I think, in the limitations of the mass mind to which I referred in Chapter 30. Even individuals of intelligence and cultivation, when they become numerous enough to constitute a mob, surrender their critical faculties, succumbing to the gravitational attraction of the mass mind that bases its assurance of truth on the assumption that what everyone says is true must be true because everyone says so.

The skeptics of the seventeenth and eighteenth centuries also had a more immediate and practical reason for favoring tolerance. Until the middle of the seventeenth century, Europe had all but destroyed itself in the religious wars by which rival ideologies (as we may call them) had each tried to extirpate the other in order to impose its own undisputed sway. For Locke, to whom the memory of the experience was still vivid, the persecution by the votaries of one religion of those who gave their allegiance to another could not succeed in establishing the universal religious conformity at which it aimed, but by compelling a like militancy and intransigeance in response it could create a wasteland of human suffering and put an end to progress in the pursuit of human betterment.

Among the Swiss cantons, religious war continued until 1848; since when the Swiss, having learned their lesson, have adopted a régime of reciprocal tolerance under which they have become what may be the least unhappy nation on earth.

To Locke and Voltaire, then, intolerance was wrong not only because those who practiced it did so on the assumption that they alone knew the truth, but also because it destroyed what makes life hopeful. Tolerance became the keystone of the liberal societies that developed after the wars of religion in consequence of the lesson taught by the experience of those wars.

In the second half of the twentieth century, however, with the increasing dominance of mass thinking, which is not able to

take account of philosophical considerations or ancient historical experience, the foundations on which the principle of tolerance rests have in some measure crumbled. Intellectual communities, themselves, have become ideological communities, as they had been from the eleventh to the seventeenth centuries. And ideology, as we have seen, excludes toleration.

38

IN THE LAST chapter I set forth the classic argument for tolerance. My justification for having done so is that, although it continues to be known to the knowing, it is increasingly disregarded as inimical to the kind of commitment advocated by Mr. Sartre, and there is a danger of its being forgotten altogether as new generations arrive to replace the old. I suspect that few of the committed students in our day would see any grounds for regarding tolerance as a virtue. They have not experienced the religious wars, even vicariously, and among the ignorant there has always been the impression that history is irrelevant to the present.

The argument against Manicheism, against what I have called the fallacy of the two species, is in harmony with the argument for tolerance. It is almost impossible to convince people who are under the influence of ideological bigotry that those whom they regard as belonging to an enemy species are human. I remember a conference at which a speaker apparently met with complete agreement when he maintained that Mr. John Foster Dulles, then the American Secretary of State, was pursuing the deliberate purpose of bringing about a nuclear war. Although never an admirer or defender of Mr. Dulles, when my turn came to speak I raised the question of why he would wish for a war in which it had to be expected that he, his wife, his children, and

his grandchildren would be burned to death. Nobody thought of an answer, but I had the impression that neither did anybody get the point. There was the kind of silent bewilderment that attends the failure of minds to meet. The explanation, I think, is that the rest of the group did not share my assumption that Mr. Dulles was a human being essentially like the rest of us, who could therefore be expected to have human reactions like our own. A young man with burning eyes came up to me afterwards, accused me of trying to destroy everything he believed in, said he would not let me do so, and then, as if I had been Mephistopheles, walked away before I would be able to answer him. He represented the commitment that is urged upon us all, the commitment that requires us not to listen to dissenting arguments.

Again I quote Dr. Niehbuhr:

> Toleration of persons who are different in kind requires an awareness of the similarities and identities above and beneath the differences; it requires an awareness of a common humanity, for instance, underneath ethnic distinctions. It is therefore a spiritual achievement of great moment. Toleration of people who differ in convictions and habits requires a residual awareness of the complexity of truth and the possibility of opposing views having some light on one or the other facet of a many-sided truth.[1]

There is another kind of commitment than that urged upon us today. It is the Socratic commitment to follow wherever the argument leads, the commitment to the kind of continuing inquiry that requires a readiness to abandon theses previously upheld if the argument goes against them. It is the commitment, in a word, to non-commitment. Here is the classic commitment of the scholar, of all those who are members of academic communities; but it has been giving way increasingly, in our time, to the ideological commitment that is its antithesis.

Finally, for those of us who are committed to the freedom

[1] Niebuhr, p. 353.

that includes the possibility of non-commitment, there is another principle of purely practical import. All the individuals who live together in a society are under a necessary discipline on which the survival of the society and its members depends. They have to abide by a common code of behavior that safeguards the rights of all and the health of the whole. In its most elementary form this means that they have to remain within certain confines of moderation, not giving free rein to their appetites, to their passions, or to the impulse to make their opinions prevail by any means over the opinions of others. If this discipline is not voluntarily maintained as self-discipline, then there is no alternative to the imposed discipline of the police state. There is either the self-discipline that prevails in a high state of civilization, or there is the terroristic discipline that is enforced from without.

In those societies that have enjoyed true freedom, its enjoyment has depended on general adherence to what one may call "the rules of the game." These rules set the limits within which debate, competition, and conflict are to be conducted. By these rules, in the more advanced democracies, the verdict of an election is accepted by the losing as by the winning side, the decisions of the courts are accepted as governing, and the laws are respected.

Certainly there are situations that nullify the obligation of members of the public to abide by the rules. If election results plainly represent manipulation by the corrupt, if judges are venal and no recourse to higher jurisdiction is possible, if the police side with the lawbreakers rather than against them, then the rules are already, in whatever degree, abandoned. If the government, usurping power, proceeds to courses of action that violate the rules in essential respects, as was the case with the government that fell under Hitler's control, there is even an obligation of rebellion. This, however, is quite different from refusing to accept a verdict of the courts simply because, dis-

agreeing with it, one considers it unjust, or from impeding the legitimate operations of government on grounds of commitment to a generalized opposition.

The old saying that the end does not justify the means is too simple by itself, but within broad limits it is basic. For the very structure of civilization is a structure of means; its discipline has to do with means rather than ends. The ordering of a free society and the conditions of its progress exist primarily as a complex of accepted means within which the people (plural) are able to pursue their common or respective ends.

Civilization, as Hobbes observed, is an artifice. Its discipline, which is necessarily artificial, consists of voluntary self-limitation to the means it provides. If, on ideological grounds, those means are flouted and their operation prevented, freedom fails and the sordid discipline of the police state takes its place. It is this consequence of which the responsible will take account in deciding how far they are justified in pursuing ends implicitly destructive of the foundations of freedom.

39

THE INDIVIDUAL MIND that thinks for itself will, in the course of its development, provide its own intellectual content, drawing on its environment at will. As for the common mind, composed of individual minds that are not prepared to provide for themselves, what serves it for content is, to a large extent, ready-made ideology or the assorted products of ideological thinking. The common mind, so provided, tends to be Manichean and intolerant. If all men, accepting the principle of commitment, should surrender their minds to one or another of the rival ideologies that contend for dominance, mankind's most precious qualities would be lost, its most hopeful possibilities

would be foreclosed, and perhaps this earth would become a stage on which mindless hordes tore each other to pieces in the name of unquestionable truth.

The dynamics of democracy in the liberal societies of the world have been involving an ever larger proportion of their populations in an ever wider range of governmental decisions, at the same time that the issues arising for decision have been growing more abstruse. In the most advanced states today, the majority of individuals pass their lives in urban concentrations of their fellow men, their senses, their minds, their nerves under bombardment by loudspeakers and headlines, finding themselves called upon to join with these millions of others or those in stopping or compelling governmental action with respect to issues of war, of peace, of military defence, of budgeting, of a thousand other matters that they lack the means to comprehend. Under such circumstances, so buffeted as they are, the exercise of individual choice becomes hardly more than a matter of choosing which among the marching and counter-marching masses to join. The individual mind is enclosed and cut off from the perspectives of the universe and history, from the natural air and the light, from what is eternal. Any attempt to keep it alive, to bring it into play, invites the charge of antisocial conduct and, perhaps, a sort of ostracism. Until now, however, there has never been a time in history when individual minds have not asserted themselves in spite of everything, and herein lies the hope of mankind.

If we appreciate the fact that none of us has any completed knowledge of what is true and right, we will not try to impose truth and righteousness on others. We will, rather, favor an organization of society that provides for continuing inquiry by maintaining an open market-place in which anyone may subject his own ideas, in competition with those of others, to the test of examination and debate. Just as biological evolution progresses by a process of natural selection that depends on a diversity of

biological forms from which to select, so cultural evolution progresses by a dialectical process of selection that depends on a like diversity of ideas from which to select. We should therefore favor an organization of society that protects diversity. We should favor it, not because it conforms to our knowledge of ultimate truth, but because it conforms to our incompletely resolved ignorance. We should favor it, not out of bigotry, but out of its opposite, a salutary skepticism.

If we appreciate the fact that none of us has any final knowledge of what is true and right, we shall be undogmatic in advancing our ideas, willing to modify or abandon them, and willing to listen to the ideas of others. In this sense and to this extent we will reject commitment, we will reject Pharisaism, we will reject Manicheism. We will oppose the exclusion of any from participation in the process of common inquiry except on grounds of unwillingness to abide by the rules of the marketplace. All that is required of those who operate in the marketplace is that they respect the rules that make such operation possible. Any commodity market in any town or village of the world operates on the same principle.

I have already recognized the fact that most persons are not prepared to bear the burden of such freedom as the market-place affords, but they are not obliged to bring any wares to market and there is nothing to prevent anyone from putting himself under the discipline of a legitimate community based on direction from above (see Chapter 25). The option of such commitment must be open to all.[1]

A commitment I do question is the common commitment to

---

[1] One of the arguments offered against a society that protects freedom and diversity is that it cannot provide adequately for the economic needs of the population. I acknowledge that any but a highly advanced people cannot operate such a society at all. If, then, we confine the issue to peoples advanced enough to enjoy this possibility, the evidence indicates that the free society is better able to provide for the economic needs of its people. We have only to compare the relative prosperity of the peoples at all levels in the free societies of Western Europe with the relative misery of those in the totalitarian societies of Eastern Europe.

raising the moral standards and enhancing the understanding of others, the commitment of the individual to teaching others what is right and true. Such a commitment has a false foundation in the assumption that one has already achieved, in one's own person, what is right and true. It seems to me that the primary concern of any individual who feels that he has a light to live by must be to live by that light himself; it must be with the constant improvement of his own performance; it must be with meeting his own standards; it must be with the level to which he is able to raise himself. Surely a man who lives his own life as well as he can may justify that life better, by the example it provides, than if he spent it in showing others how to live theirs.

This brings me to the final point I have to make. A man, I say, is responsible for himself, for what he succeeds in making of himself during the span of his life. This is so whether he lives in a society that is enjoying a golden age or in a society that has fallen into corruption and barbarism, whether he lives in the New Jerusalem or Sodom. Socrates did not encompass the salvation of the Athenian society, but in saving his own honor he saved the honor of mankind, providing the classic example of a life committed to free inquiry based on the knowledge of one's own ignorance. Boethius could not save the degenerate Roman society from the barbarism into which it had already fallen; again, however, Theodoric the Ostrogoth and all his soldiers, whatever they did to his body, could not prevent him from saving, in his own person, the honor of mankind. An all-powerful king put every pressure he could on Thomas More to dishonor himself, but in the end had to accept the alternative of putting him to death. In our own time, Milovan Djilas has manifested the Socratic compulsion to utter the truth as he sees it, even at the cost of passing the prime of his life in jail.

The saving grace afforded every individual, in whatever circumstances he finds himself, is that his honor as a man depends on himself alone. All the powers of darkness, with arma-

ment enough to blacken the whole earth, cannot put a stain on his honor. If, then, he loses his honor it can only be by his own agency. So it is that, although Athens put Socrates to death, the real victory was his. So it is that the real victor was not Henry the Eighth but Thomas More. This is the moral of Melville's *Moby Dick*, in which Ahab realizes the only victory that counts even as the white whale drags him down into the depths. It is the theme of Flecker's *Hassan*, in which the humble shopkeeper is exalted over the Caliph of Baghdad even as, in rags, he leaves the corruption of the city to go out into the desert on the endless quest.

As we face an uncertain future in which the forces of Pharisaism, of bigotry, and of ignorance may become dominant, in which the world of learning may succumb to those forces even through the agency of those who have it in their keeping, and in which the increasing disorder may evoke an increasingly sordid despotism, the saving principle remains. The primary moral responsibility of each of us is for himself alone, and though Hell itself should rise up and overspread the earth it could not take away our power to realize that responsibility.

We do not, then, have to believe those who say that the life of a man is not authentic unless he descends into the street and there sells his soul to one or the other of the bigotries that contend for it. One may be a skeptic, an agnostic, or an atheist and still believe that for every individual there is a higher commitment.

And therefore . . . come a stove boat and stove body when they will, for stave my soul, Jove himself cannot.

APPENDIX I

Readings

IN THE FOREGOING pages I have referred to the contrast between our true ignorance and the shows of knowledge behind which we are impelled to hide it. The classic statement of this is in Plato's *Apology*. If Socrates were to return in our own day and visit our learned circles in search of wisdom he would find that the situation, if more complicated, was not essentially different from what it had been in his Athens.

I am tempted to believe that it would make a difference for the future of our civilization if every highschool graduate had been made familiar with the sense of the *Apology*. Since, in fact, only a minority even of university graduates are familiar with this classic, I am including at the end of this Appendix the most relevant parts. Any reader of this book might wish to refresh his memory of these passages.

I have also referred to the Manichean illusion that mankind is divided between two species, the good and the evil. The conflict between good and evil, rather than being the inner conflict known to each of us, is regarded as a conflict between the virtuous, with whom we identify ourselves, and the wicked, whom it is our moral duty to extirpate. The two species may be the cops and the robbers, or the cowboys and the Indians, or the Ameri-

cans and the Communists, or the anti-colonialists and the imperialists, or the peace-loving nations and the aggressor nations. I have made the argument that this illusion has by itself obviated the possibility of making a genuine peace after each of the two world wars in this century.[1] I have no basic text to offer, but the following four quotations may fill the place of one.

> ... knowledge of human nature ... would have taught ... the true state of the case, that few are the good and few the evil, and that the great majority are in an intermediate class.
>
> > Socrates in Plato's *Phaedo*, translation by R. W. Livingston in *Portrait of Socrates*, London, 1938, p. 146

> The fierce and partial writers of the times, ascribing *all* virtue to themselves, and imputing *all* guilt to their adversaries, have painted the battle of the angels and daemons. Our calmer reason will reject such pure and perfect monsters of vice or sanctity, and will impute an equal, or at least an indiscriminate, measure of good and evil to the hostile sectaries, who assumed and bestowed the appellations of orthodox and heretics. . . . On either side, the error might be innocent, the faith sincere, the practice meritorious or corrupt. . . . The metaphysical opinions of the Athanasians and the Arians could not influence their moral character. . . .
>
> > Edward Gibbon, *Decline and Fall of the Roman Empire*, London, 1909, Vol. 2, Chap. XXI, pp. 390–391

> Behind the great conflicts of mankind is a terrible human predicament which lies at the heart of the story; and sooner or later the historian will base the very structure of his narrative upon it. Contemporaries fail to see the predicament or refuse to recognize its genuineness, so that our knowledge of it comes from later analysis—it is only with the progress of historical science on a particular subject that men come really to recognize that there was a terrible knot almost beyond the ingenuity of man to untie.

[1] Halle, 1962, Chap. IV and "Amplifications," Sections 14 through 18; and Halle, 1967, pp. 32–37.

It represents therefore a contribution that historical science itself has added to our interpretation of life—one which leads us to place a different construction on the whole human drama, since it uncovers the tragic element in human conflict. In historical perspective we learn to be a little more sorry for both parties than they knew how to be for one another.

> Herbert Butterfield, "The Tragic Element in Modern Conflict," in his *History and Human Relations*, London, 1951, pp. 16–17

The limitation of community, hitherto, to the scale of tribe or nation has been accompanied by a conception of mankind as divided into opposed species. The children of Yahweh have been distinguished from the children of Baal, aristocrats have been distinguished from commoners, "peace-loving nations" have been distinguished from "aggressor nations," as though the distinctions were genetic, like that between cats and dogs. The concept of the two species ("we" and "they", the good and the wicked) has dominated the history of mankind to our own present.

The logical implication of the concept is, as we have already seen, genocide. If the world is divided between the good and the wicked, then the triumph of the good implies the destruction of the wicked. "The only good Indian," said the North American pioneer, "is a dead Indian." So Yahweh destroyed the people of Sodom; so the children of Yahweh, when they captured Jericho, destroyed the children of Baal; so the representatives of the people of France put the aristocrats to the guillotine; so the Nazi regime in Germany undertook the extermination of the Jews; so we Americans were able, in 1945, to destroy the people of Hiroshima and Nagasaki.

The fact that the concept of the two species (in its various forms) implies genocide should not cause us to dismiss it if it meets our tests for the validity of nominal concepts. If we have reason to believe that it does faithfuly represent the existential reality for which it stands, then the extermination of the wicked may be an obligation of the virtuous.

In fact, however, it typifies the thinking of the immature more than that of those who have ripened in the knowledge of

existential reality and the discipline of logic. The contrast between Abraham Lincoln's attitude toward the defeated people of
the South and that of most of his fellow citizens in the victorious
North, a contrast between sophistication and simplicity, is
repeated time and again throughout history, beginning with the
eighteenth chapter of Genesis.

Similarities are not as susceptible of definition as differences
because they lend themselves less readily to the process of analy-
sis. The method of science, in a strict sense, is analytical, a
procedure of taking things apart. For putting things together,
for establishing valid associations, one depends rather on the
intuitions of the creative imagination, of the generalizing eye, as
expressed chiefly in the arts or the humanities (although
expressed under the rubric of science by a Newton or an
Einstein). This requires a greater sophistication.

"Not long ago," Clifton Fadiman wrote, "I happened to observe a mother lifting her eight-year-old boy in her arms. As she
did so she laughed and said, 'You're getting so big you'll be
lifting me soon.' It was the simplest of statements. Yet I felt
something transiently touching about the scene merely because
millions upon millions of mothers reaching back into the dawn
of history must have said the same thing to their children at
some time and because other millions will say it in the remote
future long after this mother and child are dead."

It is this recognition of oneself in others, this discovery of
experience common to all men, that contributes the moving
element in humanistic art. This, we say, is universal experience.
What the American mother said in the twentieth century a
Jewish mother said in the days of Joshua, and if the language
was different the difference was superficial only. And the
Egyptian mother who was to lose her firstborn before the prediction of his growth could come true; the Chinese mother in the
mud compound on the banks of the Yellow River, in the time of
Confucius or two thousand years later—it is all the same; the
Japanese mother in the corner of her garden under the cherry
blossoms, in the evening of too warm a day as at last the sun sinks
upon the horizon; the Viking mother on the banks of the fjord,
whose man has gone south in the longboat for the raiding season,
and who says to the little boy that he will have to be her man
now until his father comes back (wondering, as countless women

have, whether he ever will); the African mother, naked at the river's edge, placing her son astride her hip; the Roman matron or the English lady or the Macedonian peasant woman; the American Indian mother outside the tepee on the Great Plains, or my wife—all know the thought, the attitude, the emotion, the essential experience.

It is the same with Pieter Breughel's painting of a frolic at the village tavern, the children playing games, slipping between their elders' feet, getting into mischief, and half their elders merely bigger children than they—five hundred years ago as it might be today, in the low countries as it might be here. Or Vermeer's painting of the cook, the brawn of her arm pouring the milk from the pitcher as the afternoon sun comes through the kitchen window to make the scene golden—just like the peasant girl in our kitchen now, stopping to shoo away the children who want to know, eternally, when it will be ready. The scene repeats itself for thousands of years (the golden light of the sun on evenings then as now), while the individuals who enact it are replaced generation after generation, different and forever the same. Vermeer's peasant girl is taking her turn in an eternal pageant.

Or Abraham dozing at his tent door "in the heat of the day," until the unexpected approach of such honored visitors brings him to his feet, half ashamed and confused at having been found napping—and then the stir indoors where Sarah, the eternal housewife, never yet surprised, must perform the eternal feat of hospitality with briskness and laughter. (One can see old Sarah's arm pouring out the milk, like the cook's in the painting by Vermeer, like that of my wife or the girl in the kitchen now.) Or Sarah, learning that she and Abraham are to have a child of their union when they are already beyond the age for such things ("After I have grown old, and my husband is old, shall I have pleasure?"), saying: "God has made laughter for me; everyone who hears will laugh over me." This is not Jewish life in a legendary past but the life of mankind forever.

The record of history and the arts is full of such testimony. One finds it in Thoreau, or a Chinese artist of the Sung Dynasty, looking at a kingfisher. One sees it in the idealist Augustine (or Marcus Aurelius), made hopeless by the politics of his day and seeking escape in philosophy; in Hamlet's revulsion against

the nastiness of the Danish court; in Thucydides, appalled by the folly and destruction of war twenty-five centuries ago, offering his account of "the past as an aid to the interpretation of the future, which in the course of human things must resemble if it does not reflect it."

The concept of opposed species does not do justice to the basic humanity that these similarities represent. The dehumanization of the foreigner, the image of one's antagonist as a demonic being, the implicit denial that human pleasures and human sufferings, human strengths and human weaknesses, human virtues and human vices are to him as to us—this is based on an inadequate appreciation of existential reality.

> Louis J. Halle, *Men and Nations*, Princeton, 1962, One, VII, 36, pp. 108 ff.

Finally, it is worth noting that, in the Old Testament (Leviticus 19:18) and the New (Matthew 22:39), what has traditionally been mistranslated as an admonition to "love thy neighbor as thyself" is, in fact, an admonition to "love thy neighbor as a man like unto thyself."

Intimately associated with Manicheism is the Pharisaism that impels us to offer for public display a contrast between our supposed virtue and the supposed wickedness of others. This, too, takes many forms, including a denigration of others that assumes our own superiority. A compound form is that show of a putative idealism with which we dedicate ourselves to the reform or uplift of others, for it adds to the show itself the assumption that we have already attained the virtue and wisdom we now undertake to confer on the benighted. Here the basic texts are from the sayings of Jesus, chiefly the parable of the Pharisee and the publican. I give them herewith.

> And he spake this parable unto certain which trusted in themselves that they were righteous, and despised others: Two men went up into the temple to pray; the one a Pharisee,

and the other a publican. The Pharisee stood and prayed thus with himself, God, I thank thee, that I am not as other men are, extortioners, unjust, adulterers, or even as this publican. I fast twice in the week, I give tithes of all that I possess. And the publican, standing far off, would not lift up so much as his eyes unto heaven, but smote upon his breast, saying, God be merciful to me a sinner. I tell you this man went down to his house justified rather than the other.

Luke 18:9–14 (Authorized Version)

Be careful not to make a show of your religion before men; if you do, no reward awaits you in your Father's house in heaven.

Thus, when you do some act of charity, do not announce it with a flourish of trumpets, as the hypocrites do in synagogue and in the streets to win admiration from men. I tell you this: they have their reward already. No; when you do some act of charity, do not let your left hand know what your right is doing; your good deed must be secret, and your Father who sees what is done in secret will reward you.

Again, when you pray, do not be like the hypocrites; they love to say their prayers standing up in synagogue and at the street-corners, for everyone to see them. I tell you this; they have their reward already. But when you pray, go into a room by yourself, shut the door, and pray to your Father who is there in the secret place; and your Father who sees what is secret will reward you.

Matthew 6:1–6 (New English Bible)

The scribes and the Pharisees brought a woman who had been caught in adultery, and placing her in the midst they said to him, "Teacher, this woman has been caught in the act of adultery. Now in the law Moses commanded us to stone such. What do you say about her?" This they said to test him, that they might have some charge to bring against him. Jesus bent down and wrote with his finger on the ground. And as they continued to ask him, he stood up and said to them, "Let him who is without sin among you be the first to throw a stone at her."

John 8:3–9 (Revised Standard Version)

SOME OBSERVATIONS BY SOCRATES

Socrates, aged seventy, was brought to trial before a jury of five hundred Athenians in an open-air court. The charges, made by one Meletus, were (1) that he was guilty of not believing in the gods in whom the state believed, and (2) that he was also guilty of corrupting the minds of the young. The *Apology* is the speech Socrates made to the jury in his own defence, as Plato recalled it.

The following selections are taken from the translation by R. W. Livingstone in the little volume of Plato's three dialogues dealing with the death of Socrates entitled *Portrait of Socrates*, Oxford, 1938, by permission of the Clarendon Press.

5. I daresay, Athenians, that some one among you will reply, "Yes, Socrates, but what is the origin of these accusations which are brought against you? There must have been something strange which you have been doing. All these rumours and this talk about you would never have arisen if you had been like other men: tell us, then, what is the cause of them, for we should be sorry to judge hastily of you." Now I regard this as a fair challenge, and I will endeavour to explain to you the reason why I have got this name and this bad reputation. Please to attend then. And although some of you may think that I am joking, I declare that I will tell you the entire truth. Men of Athens, this reputation of mine has come of a certain sort of wisdom which I possess. If you ask me what kind of wisdom, I reply, the wisdom which, I think, belongs to man; for to that extent I am inclined to believe that I am wise, whereas the persons of whom I was speaking [certain sophists: i.e., professional wise men or teachers] have a superhuman wisdom, which I may fail to describe, because I have it not myself; and he who says that I have, speaks falsely, and is taking away my character. And here, men of Athens, I must beg you not to interrupt me, even if I seem to say something extravagant. For the word which I will speak is not mine. I will refer you to a witness who is worthy of credit; that witness shall be the God of Delphi—he will tell you about my wisdom, if I have any, and

of what sort it is. You must have known Chaerephon; he was early a friend of mine, and also a friend of yours, for he shared in the recent exile of the people, and returned with you. Well, Chaerephon, as you know, was very impetuous in all his doings, and he went to Delphi and boldly asked the oracle to tell him whether—as I was saying, I must beg you not to interrupt—he asked the oracle to tell him whether any one was wiser than I was, and the Pythian prophetess answered, that there was no man wiser. Chaerephon is dead himself; but his brother, who is in court, will confirm the truth of what I am saying.

6. Why do I mention this? Because I am going to explain to you why I have such an evil name. When I heard the answer, I said to myself, What can the god mean, and what is the interpretation of his riddle? for I know that I have no wisdom, small or great. What then can he mean when he says that I am the wisest of men? And yet he is a god, and cannot lie; that would be against his nature. After great hesitation, I thought of the following method of trying the question. I reflected that if I could only find a man wiser than myself, then I might go to the god with a refutation in my hand. I should say to him, "Here is a man who is wiser than I am; but you said that I was the wisest." Accordingly I went to one who had the reputation of wisdom, and observed him—his name I need not mention; he was a politician whom I selected for examination—and the result was as follows: When I began to talk with him, I could not help thinking that he was not really wise, although he was thought wise by many, and still wiser by himself; and thereupon I tried to explain to him that he thought himself wise, but was not really wise; and the consequence was that he hated me, and his enmity was shared by several who were present and heard me. So I left him, saying to myself, as I went away: Well, although I do not suppose that either of us knows anything really beautiful and good, I am better off than he is—for he knows nothing, and thinks that he knows; I neither know nor think that I know. In this one point then I seem to have the advantage of him. Then I went to another who had still higher pretensions to wisdom, and my conclusion was exactly the same. Whereupon I made another enemy of him.

7. Then I went to one man after another, becoming conscious of the enmity which I provoked, and it distressed and alarmed me: but necessity was laid upon me—the word of God, I thought, ought to be considered first. And I said to myself, Go I must to all who appear to know, and find out the meaning of the oracle. And I swear to you, Athenians, by the dog I swear!—for I must tell you the truth—the result of my mission was just this: I found that the men most in repute were all but the most foolish; and that others less esteemed were really wiser and better. I will tell you the tale of my wanderings and of the "Herculean" labours, as I may call them, which I endured only to find at last the oracle irrefutable. After the politicians, I went to the poets—tragic, dithyrambic, and all sorts. And there, I said to myself, you will be instantly detected; now you will find out that you are more ignorant than they are. Accordingly, I took them some of the most elaborate passages in their own writings, and asked what was the meaning of them—thinking that they would teach me something. Will you believe me? I am almost ashamed to confess the truth, but I must say that there was hardly a person present who would not have talked better about their poetry than they did themselves. Then I soon discovered that not by wisdom do poets write poetry, but by a natural gift and inspiration; they are like diviners or soothsayers who also say many fine things, but do not understand the meaning of them. The poets appeared to me to be in much the same case; and I further observed that upon the strength of their poetry they believed themselves to be the wisest of men in other things in which they were not wise. So I departed, conceiving myself to be superior to them for the same reason that I was superior to the politicians.

8. At last I went to the artisans, for I was conscious that I knew nothing at all, as I may say, and I was sure that they knew many fine things; and here I was not mistaken, for they did know many things of which I was ignorant, and in this they certainly were wiser than I was. But I observed that even the good artisans fell into the same error as the poets—because they were good workmen they thought that they also knew all sorts of high matters, and this defect in them overshadowed their wisdom; and therefore I asked myself on behalf of the oracle, whether I

would like to be as I was, having neither their knowledge nor their ignorance, or like them in both; and I made answer to myself and to the oracle that I was better off as I was.

9. This inquisition has led to my having many enemies of the worst and most dangerous kind, and has given occasion also to many calumnies. And I am called wise, for my hearers always imagine that I myself possess the wisdom which I find wanting in others: but the truth is, men of Athens, that God only is wise; and by his answer he intends to show that the wisdom of men is worth little or nothing; he is not speaking of Socrates, he is only using my name by way of illustration, as if he said, He is the wisest, who, like Socrates, knows that his wisdom is in truth worth nothing. . . .

16. . . . Some one will say: And are you not ashamed, Socrates, of a course of life which is likely to bring you to an untimely end? To him I may fairly answer: There you are mistaken: a man who is good for anything ought not to calculate the chance of living or dying; he ought only to consider whether in doing anything he is doing right or wrong—acting the part of a good man or of a bad. . . . Wherever a man's place is, whether the place which he has chosen or that in which he has been placed by his commander, there he ought to remain in the hour of danger; he should not think of death or of anything but of disgrace. . . .

17. . . . For the fear of death is indeed the pretence of wisdom, and not real wisdom, being a pretence of knowing the unknown; and no one knows whether death, which men in their fear apprehend to be the greatest evil, may not be the greatest good. Is not this ignorance of a disgraceful sort, the ignorance which is the conceit that a man knows what he does not know? And in this respect only I believe myself to differ from men in general, and may perhaps claim to be wiser than they are:—that whereas I know but little of the next world, I do not suppose that I know; but I do know that injustice and disobedience to a better, whether God or man, is evil and ugly, and I will never fear or fly what for all I know may be good rather than what I am certain is evil. And therefore if you let me go now, and are not convinced by Anytus, who said that since I had been prosecuted I must be put to death; (or if not, that I ought never to have

been prosecuted at all); and that if I escape now, your sons will all be utterly ruined by listening to my words—if you say to me, Socrates, this time we will not mind Anytus, and you shall be let off, but upon one condition, that you are not to inquire and speculate in this way any more, and that if you are caught doing so again you shall die;—if this was the condition on which you let me go, I should reply: Men of Athens, I have the warmest affection for you; but I shall obey God rather than you, and while I have life and strength I shall never cease from the practice and teaching of philosophy. . . . And so, men of Athens, I say to you, do as Anytus bids or not as Anytus bids, and either acquit me or not; but whichever you do, understand that I shall never alter my ways, not even if I have to die many times.

19. . . . I am certain, men of Athens, that if I had engaged in politics, I should have perished long ago, and done no good either to you or to myself. And do not be offended at my telling you the truth: for the truth is, that no man who opposes you or any other crowd and tries to prevent the many unjust and illegal acts which are done in the state, will save his life. . . .

I conclude this series of quotations with one that exemplifies the Socratic recognition of one's own limitations together with the transcendence of Manicheism and Pharisaism alike. It is the more remarkable because its context was a direct debate between candidates for public office, and its theme was an issue over which public passion had risen so high among the American people that it was shortly to break out in civil war. In a debate of August 21, 1858, with his rival for the office of Senator from Illinois, Stephen A. Douglas, Abraham Lincoln said about the people of the South:

They are just what we would be in their situation. If slavery did not now exist among them, they would not introduce it. If it did now exist among us, we should not instantly give it up. This I believe of the masses North and South. Doubtless there are individuals on both sides who would not hold slaves under any circumstances; and others who would gladly introduce slavery anew, if it were out of existence. . . . When Southern people tell us they are no more responsible for the origin of slavery than

we, I acknowledge the fact. When it is said that the institution exists, and that it is very difficult to get rid of it in any satisfactory way, I can understand and appreciate the saying. I surely will not blame them for not doing what I should not know how to do myself. If all earthly power were given me, I should not know what to do as to the existing institution.

Later, as President of the United States and as commander-in-chief of the Northern forces in the Civil War, Lincoln showed the same spirit and the same attitude in his Second Inaugural Address, delivered on March 4, 1865, a month and ten days before he was killed by an assassin whose motive was rooted in Manicheism.

APPENDIX II

Foreign Language Citations

BECAUSE NO translation expresses an author's thought in his own words, the translations into English quoted in the text are presented here in their original languages, with two exceptions: (1) The *Manifesto of the Communist Party* by Marx and Engels, as translated by Samuel Moore with the collaboration of Engels, is an historical document in its own right, accepted by Marxists as a fully authoritative text. It would therefore be supererogatory to give the original German version of quotations from it as a means of checking upon them. (2) What is true of the *Manifesto* is less true of Lenin's *The State and Revolution*, although the English translation quoted is still authoritative as some unauthorized individual's casual translation would not be. Here, moreover, as in the case of the quotation from Dosteyevsky, the fact that fewer readers of English are able to read the Russian in which it was originally written than French or German was an additional consideration.

Except for the translations from the French, which are my own, the authors of the translations into English quoted in the text are given in the List of Publications.

Page v
Die Gedanken, welche diese Schrift enthält, können bei ihrer

öffentlichen Äusserung keinen andern Zweck noch Wirkung haben, als das Verstehen dessen, was ist, und damit die ruhigere Ansicht sowie ein in der wirklichen Berührung und in Worten gemässigtes Ertragen derselben zu befördern.

> Hegels Sämtliche Werke, Band VII, *Schriften zur Politik und Rechtsphilosophie*, Hrsg. Georg Lasson, 1913, 2. durchgesehene Auflage 1923, Leipzig, p. 5.

Preface, page viii
Haec omnia inde esse in quibusdam vera, unde in quibusdam falsa sunt.

> St. Augustine of Hippo, quoted by Kaufmann, 1966, p. 67.

4, *page* 16
Ἐκ τούτων οὖν φανερὸν ὅτι τῶν φύσει ἡ πόλις ἐστί, καὶ ὅτι ἄνθρωπος φύσει πολιτικὸν ζῷον.

> Aristotle, *ΠΟΛΙΤΙΚΩΝ Α*, 1253a.

4, *page* 17
Puisqu'il n'y a rien plus grand en terre après Dieu, que les princes souverains, et qu'ils sont établis de lui comme ses lieutenants, pour commander aux autres hommes, il est besoin de prendre garde à leur qualité, afin de respecter et reverer leur majesté en toute obéissance, sentir et parler d'eux en tout honneur: car qui méprise son prince souverain, il méprise Dieu, duquel il est l'image en terre.

6, *page* 27
Chacun de nous met en commun sa personne et toute sa puissance sous la suprême direction de la volonté générale; et nous recevons encore chaque membre comme partie indivisible du tout.

. . . l'aliénation totale de chaque associé avec tous ses droits à toute la communauté.

6, *page* 27
Celui qui ose entreprendre d'instituer un peuple doit se sentir en état de changer pour ainsi dire la nature humaine, de transformer chaque individu, qui par lui-même est un tout parfait et solitaire,

en partie d'un plus grand tout dont cet individu reçoive en quelque sorte sa vie et son être; d'alterer la constitution de l'homme pour la renforcer; de substituer une existence partielle et morale à l'existence physique et indépendante que nous avons reçue de la nature. Il faut, en un mot, qu'il ôte à l'homme ses forces propres pour lui en donner qui lui soient étrangères, et dont il ne puisse faire usage sans le secours d'autrui.

6, *page* 29
... ni trop grand pour pouvoir être bien gouverné, ni trop petit pour pouvoir se maintenir par lui-même.

7, *page* 30
Il y a souvent bien de la différence entre la volonté de tous et la volonté générale.

7, *page* 31
... la volonté générale est toujours droite èt tend toujours à l'utilité publique. . . .

De lui-même, le peuple veut toujours le bien, mais de lui-même il ne le voit pas toujours.

7, *page* 31
La volonté générale est toujours droite, mais le jugement qui la guide n'est pas toujours éclairé. Il faut lui faire voir les objets tels qu'ils sont, quelquefois tels qu'ils doivent lui paroître, lui montrer le bon chemin qu'elle cherche. . . .

8, *page* 33
Les particuliers voient le bien qu'ils rejettent; le public veut le bien qu'il ne voit pas. Tous ont également besoin de guides. Il faut obliger les uns à conformer leurs volontés à leur raison; il faut apprendre à l'autre à connoître ce qu'il veut. Alors des lumières publiques résulte l'union de l'entendement et de la volonté dans le corps social; de là l'exact concours des parties, et enfin la plus grande force du tout. Voilà d'où naît la nécessité d'un législateur.

Pour découvrir les meilleures règles de société qui conviennent aux nations, il faudroit une intelligence supérieure qui vît toutes les passions des hommes, et qui n'en éprouvât aucune; qui n'eût aucun rapport avec notre nature, et qui la connût à fond; dont le

bonheur fût indépendant de nous, et qui pourtant voulût bien s'occuper du nôtre; enfin, qui, dans le progrès des temps se ménageant une gloire éloignée, pût travailler dans un siècle et jouir dans un autre. Il faudroit des dieux pour donner des lois aux hommes.

8, *page* 34
Dans la naissance des sociétés, dit Montesquieu, ce sont les chefs des républiques qui font l'institution, et c'est ensuite l'institution qui forme les chefs des républiques.

9, *page* 35
C'est vraiment une obsession chez Rousseau qu'il faut faire cesser le conflit par quoi l'homme est déchiré, donner l'homme tout entier à l'État—et c'est le *Contrat Social*—ou le laisser tout entier a lui-même: c'est *L'Émile*.

9, *page* 36
... quiconque refusera d'obéir à la volonté générale, y sera contraint par tout le corps: ce qui ne signifie autre chose sinon qu'on le forcera à être libre. ...

9, *page* 37
Fade louange d'un vil factieux et d'un prêtre absurde que tu détestes dans ton coeur.

9, *page* 38
... tant que l'amour de la patrie et de la liberté ne sera pas éteint parmi nous jamais la mémoire de ce grand homme ne cessera d'y être en bénédiction.

10, *page* 41
Je forme une entreprise qui n'eut jamais d'exemple, et dont l'exécution n'aura point d'imitateur. Je veux montrer à mes semblables un homme dans toute la vérité de la nature; et cet homme, ce sera moi. Moi seul. Je sens mon coeur et je connais les hommes. Je ne suis fait comme aucun de ceux que j'ai vus; j'ose croire n'être fait comme aucun de ceux qui existent.

10, *page* 42

Être éternel, rassemble autour de moi l'innombrable foule de mes semblables: qu'ils écoutent mes confessions, qu'ils gémissent de mes indignités, qu'ils rougissent de mes miséres.

11, *page* 43

Oh Monsieur, si j'avais jamais pû écrire le quart de ce que j'ai vû et senti sous cet arbre, avec quelle clarté j'aurais fait voir toutes les contradictions du système social, avec quelle force j'aurais exposé tous les abus de nos institutions, avec quelle simplicité j'aurais démontré que l'homme est bon naturellement et que c'est par ces institutions seules que les hommes deviennent méchants.

11, *page* 45

Товарищество поэтому не намѣрено навязывать народу какую бы то ни было организацію сверху. Будущая организація безъ сомнѣнія выработается изъ народнаго движенія и жизни, но это—дѣло будущихъ поколѣній. Наше дѣло—страшное, полное, повсемѣстное и безпощадное разрушеніе.

11, *page* 46

...während in der kommunistischen Gesellschaft, wo Jeder nicht einen ausschliesslichen Kreis der Tätigkeit hat, sondern sich in jedem beliebigen Zweige ausbilden kann, die Gesellschaft die allgemeine Produktion regelt und mir eben dadurch möglich macht, heute dies, morgen jenes zu tun, morgens zu jagen, nachmittags zu fischen, abends Viehzucht zu treiben, nach dem Essen zu kritisieren, wie ich gerade Lust habe, ohne je Jäger, Fischer, Hirt oder Kritiker zu werden.

13, *page* 51

Gott ist nur Gott, insofern er sich selber weiss; sein Sichwissen ist ferner sein Selbstbewusstsein im Menschen und das Wissen des Menschen *von* Gott, das fortgeht zum Sichwissen des Menschen *in* Gott. . . .

14, *page* 55

Das alles steht nun auf und hat zwei Beine
Und eine Brust, den Lebensfluch zu fassen!
Ha! flechten muss ich mich ans Flammenrad.
Im Kreis der Ewigkeiten Lust zu tanzen!
Gäb's ausser ihr ein Etwas, das verschlänge,
Ich spräng' hinein, müsst' ich 'ne Welt zertrümmern,
Die zwischen ihr und mir sich aufgetürmt!
Zerschelln müsst' sie am langgedehnten Fluche.
. . .

14, *page* 56

. . . Der zweite Akt ist die europäische, die Weltrevolution, der
grosse Zweikampf der Besitzlosen mit der Aristokratie des
Besitzes. . . . Wilde, düstere Zeiten dröhnen heran, und der Prophet,
der eine neue Apokalypse schreiben wollte, müsste ganz neue
Bestien erfinden, und zwar so erschreckliche, dass die älteren
Johanneischen Tiersymbole dagegen nur sanfte Täubchen und
Amoretten wären.

14, *page* 56

Der heilige Kirchenvater wird sich doch sehr wundern, wenn der
jüngste Tag, an dem sich dies alles erfüllet, über ihn hereinbricht—
ein Tag, dessen Morgenrot der Widerschein brennender Städte am
Himmel ist, wenn unter diesen 'himmlichen Harmonien' die
Melodien der "Marseillaise" und der "Carmagnole" mit obligatem
Kanondonner an sein Ohr hallt, und die Guillotine dazu den
Takt schlägt; wenn die verruchte "Masse" ça ira, ça ira brüllt und
das "Selbstbewusstsein" vermittels der Laterne aufhebt.

18, *page* 67

. . . dass er alles vernichten will, was nicht fähig ist, als Privateigentum von allen besessen zu werden; er will auf gewaltsame Weise
von Talent etc. abstrahieren. Der physische unmittelbare Besitz
gilt ihm als einziger Zweck des Lebens und Daseins; . . . das
Verhältnis des Privateigentums bleibt das Verhältnis der Gemeinschaft zur Sachenwelt; endlich spricht sich diese Bewegung, dem
Privateigentum das allgemeine Privateigentum entgegenzustellen,
in der tierischen Form aus, dass der Ehe (welche allerdings eine

Form des exklusiven Privateigentum ist) die Weibergemeinschaft, wo also das Weib zu einem gemeinschaftlichen und gemeinen Eigentum wird, entgegengestellt wird. ... Wie das Weib aus der Ehe in die allgemeine Prostitution, so tritt die ganze Welt des Reichtums, d.h. des gegenständlichen Wesens des Menschen, aus dem Verhältnis der exklusiven Ehe mit dem Privateigentümer in das Verhältnis der universellen Prostitution mit der Gemeinschaft. ... Der allgemeine und als Macht sich konstituierende Neid ist nur die versteckte Form, in welcher die Habsucht sich herstellt und nur auf eine andere Weise sich befriedigt. ... Der rohe Kommunist ist nur die Vollendung dieses Neides und dieser Nivellierung von dem vorgestellten Minimum aus. ...

In dem Verhältnis zum Weib, als dem Raub und der Magd der gemeinschaftlichen Wollust, ist die unendliche Degradation ausgesprochen, in welcher der Mensch für sich selbst existiert ...

... darum als vollständige, bewusst und innerhalb des ganzen Reichtums der bisherigen Entwicklung gewordne Rückkehr des Menschen für sich als eines gesellschaftlichen, d.h. menschlichen Menschen.

18, *page* 68
Dieser Kommunismus ist als vollendeter Naturalismus = Humanismus, als vollendeter Humanismus = Naturalismus, er ist die wahrhafte Auflösung des Widerstreites zwischen dem Menschen mit der Natur und mit dem Menschen, die wahre Auflösung des Streits zwischen Existenz und Wesen, zwischen Vergegenständlichung und Selbstbestätigung, zwischen Freiheit und Notwendigkeit, zwischen Individuum und Gattung. Er ist das aufgelöste Rätsel der Geschichte und weiss sich als diese Lösung.

18, *page* 69
Zwischen der kapitalistischen und der Kommunistischen Gesellschaft liegt die Periode der revolutionären Umwandlung der einen in die andre. Der entspricht auch eine politische Übergangsperiode, deren Staat nichts andres sein kann als *die revolutionäre Diktatur des Proletariats.*

18, *page* 70
... und die Gesellschaft auf ihre Fahne schreiben: "Jeder nach seinen Fähigkeiten, jedem nach seinen Bedürfnissen!"

20, *page* 77

Ich arbeite wie toll die Nächte durch an der Zusammenfassung meiner Ökonomischen Studien, damit ich wenigstens die Grundrisse im klaren habe bevor dem déluge.

21, *page* 79

... dass ich als nächsten Versuch der Französischen Revolution ausspreche, nicht mehr wie bisher die bürokratisch-militärische Maschine aus einer Hand in die andre zu übertragen, sondern sie zu *zerbrechen,* und dies ist die Vorbedingung jeder wirklichen Volksrevolution auf dem Kontinent.

22, *page* 82

Der erste Akt, worin der Staat wirklich als Repräsentant der ganzen Gesellschaft auftritt—die Besitzergreifung der Produktionsmittel im Namen der Gesellschaft—ist zugleich sein letzter selbständiger Akt als Staat. Das Eingreifen einer Staatsgewalt in gesellschaftliche Verhältnisse wird auf einem Gebiete nach dem andern überflüssig und schläft dann von selbst ein. An die Stelle der Regierung über Personen tritt die Verwaltung von Sachen und die Leitung von Produktionsprozessen. Der Staat wird nicht "abgeschafft," *er stirbt ab.*

23, *page* 85

Die Philosophen haben die Welt nur verschieden *interpretiert*; es kommt aber darauf an, sie zu *verändern.*

26, *page* 97

... alle Vorstellung, welcher Art sie auch sei, alles Objekt, ist Erscheinung. Ding an sich aber ist allein der Wille: als solcher ist er durchaus nicht Vorstellung, sondern toto genere von ihr verschieden: er ist es, wovon alle Vorstellung, alles Objekt, die Erscheinung, die Sichtbarkeit, die Objektität ist. Er ist das Innerste, der Kern jedes Einzelnen und ebenso des Ganzen: er erscheint in jeder blindwirkenden Naturkraft: er auch erscheint im überlegten Handeln des Menschen; welcher beiden grosse Verschiedenheit doch nur den Grad des Erscheinens, nicht das Wesen des Erscheinenden trifft.

List of Publications

THE FOLLOWING list comprises all publications cited in the text except works like the books of the Bible or the plays of Shakespeare, which require no further aid to identification than their names.

Aristotle, *Politics*, in complete works edited by Becker and Brandis, Berlin, 1831–1870.

Bodin, Jean, *Les six livres de la République*, Paris, 1578.

Bottomore, T. B., *Karl Marx: Early Writings*, London, 1963.

Butterfield, Herbert, *History and Human Relations*, London, 1951.

Carr, E. H., *Michael Bakunin*, London, 1937.

Cassirer, Ernst, *Rousseau, Kant, Goethe*, Princeton, 1970.

Donnelly, Desmond, *Struggle for the World*, London, 1965.

Dostoyevsky, Fyodor, *Crime and Punishment*, translated by Constance Garnett, New York, 1932.

Dragomanov, M. P., editor, *Pis'ma M. A. Bakunina k A. I. Gercenu i N. P. Ogarevu*, Geneva, 1896.

Eastman, Max, editor, *Capital, The Communist Manifesto, and other Writings by Karl Marx*, New York, 1932.

Engels, Friedrich, *Herrn Eugen Dührings Umwälzung der Wissenschaft*, in *Marx-Engels—Werke*, vol. 20, Berlin, 1962. English translation as *The Anti-Dühring*, Moscow, 1959.

Farbman, Michael S., *Bolshevism in Retreat*, London, 1923.

Fischer, Louis, *The Life of Lenin*, New York, 1964.

Fontaine, André, *La Guerre Froide*, Paris, 1966, 1967.

Fromm, Erich, *Marx's Concept of Man*, New York, 1961.

Gibbon, Edward, *Decline and Fall of the Roman Empire*, London, 1909.

Gissing, George, *The Private Papers of Henry Ryecroft*, New York, 1961.

Halle, Louis J., *Men and Nations*, Princeton, 1962.

——, *The Society of Man*, London and New York, 1965.

——, *The Cold War as History*, London and New York, 1967.

Hegel, G. W. F., *Grundrisse zum Gebrauch seiner Vorlesungen*, (*Enzyklopädie der philosophischen Wissenschaften, III*), Frankfurt am Main, 1970.

——, *Schriften zur Politik und Rechtsphilosophie*, Leipzig, 1913–1923.

Heine, Heinrich, *Sämtliche Werke*, Band 9, Leipzig, 1910.

Hobbes, Thomas, *Leviathan*, Oxford, 1957.

Huizinga, J., *Erasmus of Rotterdam*, New York, 1924.

Jouvenel, Bertrand de, editor, *Rousseau's Du Contrat Social*, Geneva, 1947.

Kaufmann, Walter, *Hegel: Reinterpretation, Texts, and Commentary*, London, 1966.

——, *The Owl and the Nightingale*, London, 1959.

Kennan, George F., "The Sources of Soviet Conduct," *Foreign Affairs*, July 1947.

Lenin, N., *Gosudarstvo i revolyutsiya*, Petrograd, 1917. English translation as *The State and Revolution*, London, 1919.

Mailer, Norman, *The Armies of the Night*, New York, 1968.

Marx, Karl Heinrich, *Oulanem*, in *MEGA (Marx-Engels-Gesamtausgabe)* I, 1 (2), Berlin, 1929.

——, *Ökonomisch-philosophische Manuskripte*, in *MEGA*, I, 3, Berlin, 1932.

——, *Zur Judenfrage*, in *Marx-Engels-Werke*, Vol. 2, Berlin, 1962.

——, *Thesen über Feuerbach*, in *Marx-Engels-Werke*, Vol. 3, Berlin, 1962.

——, *La Misère de la philosophie*, Paris, 1947. English translation as *The Poverty of Philosophy*, Moscow (no date given) and London, 1956.

——, with Friedrich Engels, *Manifest der Kommunistischen Partei*, in *Marx-Engels-Werke*, Vol. 4, Berlin, 1959. Translated from the original German by Samuel Moore, London, 1888.

——, with Friedrich Engels, *Deutsche Ideologie*, in *Marx-Engels-Werke*, Vol. 3, Berlin, 1962 i.

——, with Friedrich Engels, *Briefe*, in *Marx-Engels-Werke*, Vol. 29, Berlin, 1963, and Vol. 33, Berlin, 1966. English translation in

Correspondence 1846–1895: a Selection with Commentary and Notes, London, 1934.

————, *Kritik des Gothaer Programms*, in *Marx-Engels-Werke*, Vol. 19, Berlin, 1962 ii.

Niebuhr, Reinhold, "Tolerance," in *Collier's Encyclopedia*, Vol. 22, New York, 1966.

Orwell, George, *Nineteen Eighty-Four*, London, 1949.

Payne, Robert, *Marx*, London, 1968.

Rousseau, Jean-Jacques, *Discours sur les arts et les sciences*, 1750.

————, *Discours sur l'inégalité*, 1753.

————, *Du Contrat Social*, 1762.

————, *Émile*, 1762.

————, *Confessions*, 1782.

————, *Oeuvres complètes*, I, Paris, 1959.

Schopenhauer, Arthur, *Die Welt als Wille und Vorstellung*, 1844. English translation as *The World as Will and Idea*, in *The Philosophy of Schopenhauer*, Irwin Edman, editor, New York, 1928.

Tocqueville, Alexis de, *De la Démocratie en Amérique*, Paris, 1961.

Tucker, Robert C., *Philosophy and Myth in Karl Marx*, Cambridge, 1961.

Wilson, Edmund, *To the Finland Station*, New York, 1940.

Wolfe, Bertram D., *Three Who Made a Revolution*, Boston, 1948.

Index

Since this is not a book of information presented for its own sake, the following index will be useful chiefly in helping the reader return to particular remarks, citations, or passages. The Table of Contents at the front, briefly identifying the subject of each chapter, should also serve this purpose.

171

D0915404